FOR HANNE

I want to thank the following persons for their support in creating this book – Don Hahn, Yasutaka Shinozaki, Toshio Ishibashi, Maggie Gisel, Dale Kennedy, Lella Smith, Vivian Procopio, and Rosemarie Soriaga.

If you are interested in more information, go to my blog at www.its-a-wrap.blogspot.com.

HANS P BACHER

DREAM WORLDS

PRODUCTION DESIGN IN ANIMATION

ELSEVIER

Amsterdam • Boston • Heidelberg • London • New York • Oxford •
Paris • San Diego • San Francisco • Singapore • Sydney • Tokyo
Focal Press is an imprint of Elsevier

Focal Press

Acquisitions Editor: Georgia Kennedy
Publishing Services Manager: George Morrison
Senior Project Manager: Paul Gottehrer
Marketing Manager: Rebecca Pease

Focal Press is an imprint of Elsevier
30 Corporate Drive, Suite 400, Burlington, MA 01803, USA
Linacre House, Jordan Hill, Oxford OX2 8DP, UK

 Recognizing the importance of preserving what has been written, Elsevier prints its books on acid-free paper whenever possible.

Library of Congress Cataloging-in-Publication Data
Application submitted.

British Library Cataloguing-in-Publication Data
A catalogue record for this book is available from the British Library.

ISBN: 978-0-240-52093-3

For information on all Focal Press publications
visit our website at www.books.elsevier.com

08 09 10 11 5 4 3 2

Printed in China

Once upon a time in a parking lot at Universal Studios in Hollywood, California sat a small trailer – the kind of seedy temporary office space that elementary schools use when they are out of classroom space. Hans Bacher sat at a drafting table deep inside, bathed in cigarette smoke and Magic Marker fumes strong enough to kill a lesser man. He was working to flesh out the bones of a film called *Who Framed Robert Rabbit*. People like Bob Zemeckis, Chuck Jones, Steven Spielberg, and Richard Williams would make the trip back to the trailers to smell the markers and see what Hans and others (like the great storyman Joe Ranft) had come up with for Roger, Jessica, and Baby Herman.

Hans was always the kind of artist I wanted to get in early in pre-production. You could build an entire film on the shoulders of his inspiring visual development work. Ask anybody who has worked with him and they'll use the same ten words to describe his genius: hardest working, opinionated, brilliant, opinionated, the most knowledgeable, and opinionated. He is also opinionated. Don't misunderstand. You really really want his opinion.

Years after *Who Framed Roger Rabbit*, I was driving down a dirt road in France's Loire Valley with Hans as my navigator. We were scouting locations for *Beauty and the Beast*, driving fast, stopping for beer, taking pictures, and learning how to curse in German. His work on *Beauty and the Beast* set an unforgettable epic style for the film. His attention to detail and research is both expansive and surgically focused. He has every book, every photo, every graphic novel, every film on every topic, and if he doesn't, he knows who has it or how to get it within 24 hours.

He has helped set the style for so many memorable animated films from *The Lion King* to his exquisite production design on *Mulan*. For years he has shared his encyclopedic knowledge of animation and filmmaking with his students and collaborators behind the doors of the universities and film studios that were lucky enough to get him. Now for the first time in this book, you can take a peek into the mind of this amazing designer and my good friend Hans Bacher.

Enjoy.

Don Hahn
Producer
Beauty and the Beast
The Lion King

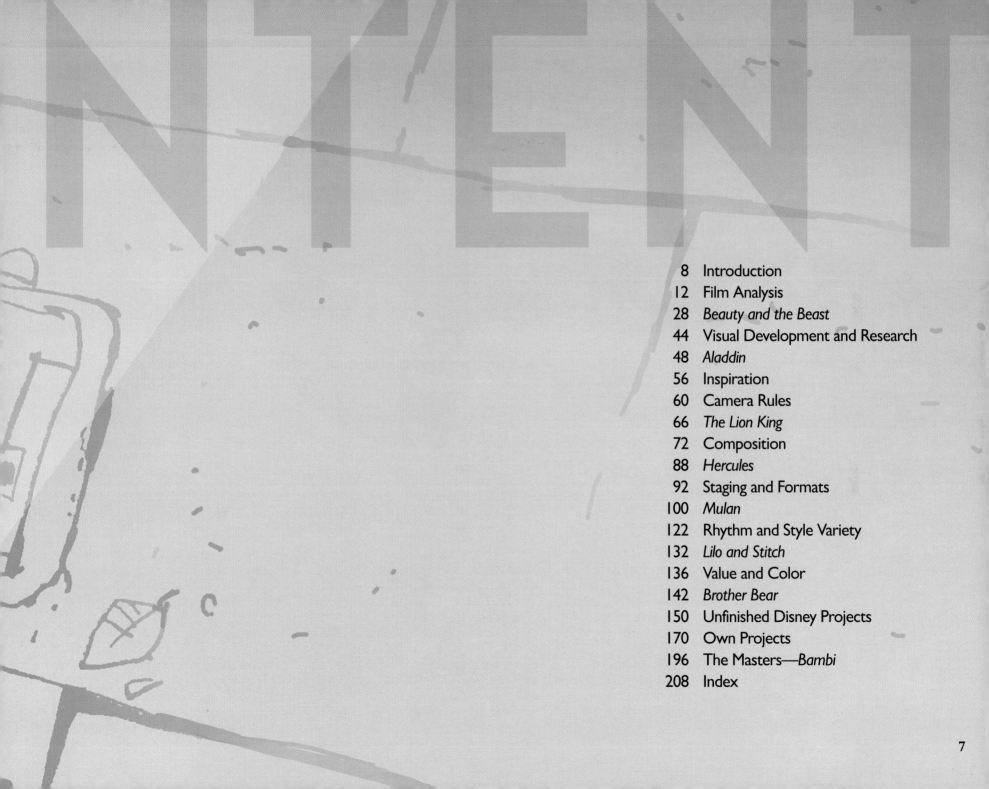

Working with film is challenging as you are creating thousands of pictures. They are all connected throughout a story with several actors: human or animals, cartoony, realistic or very stylized and, with lots of emotions, action and fantastic worlds. You are part of a creation process in which a dream world comes alive. It is scary and fascinating at the same time. So many artists create one piece of art that you alone would never be able to do.

What does it mean – Production Design? Exactly that, the design of the production; the "look" of the film. Of course, the Production Designer does not do all that independently. The vision of the director gives him or her a direction of where to go, and they are limited to a budget and a timeframe. Not to forget, the final look of the movie depends on the ability of a good design team of layout artists and background painters, who have to

translate all the ideas. A feature film is the team effort of up to sixty artists in that department. If the production designer and the art director fail to keep the quality standards up, it could end in disaster. Usually a lot of major problems have to be solved. The movie has to look expensive, but should not be expensive to produce. During the production of *Mulan*, the executives asked me constantly if we could add a bit more detail in the backgrounds.

The overall look of the film was in their opinion "poor." We were not using tonal mattes on the characters. Well, they did not use them in *Lady and the Tramp* and it did not look cheap! There is usually a lot of fighting against windmills, and in case if in the end, it looks like different pieces of the movie don't fit together, it shows that the designers lost the battle against the "powers."

I've always enjoyed working with so much talent, to get inspired and excited together with artists from very diverse disciplines. The preproduction time on a new movie in the very beginning is the best time. With complete artistic freedom, the assigned team creates the craziest and most fantastic ideas in beautiful sketches and paintings. Later, after production starts, fun is limited. Work has to happen within clear, defined borders. There are deadlines and the footage numbers become more important.

This is not a fast process. Sometimes it takes five or more years from the first ideas to the finished product.

In this book, I will try to explain the design process, show you a lot of examples and will also analyze some art pieces of the "masters." I hope you enjoy them.

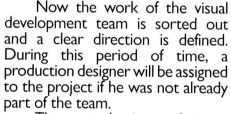

© Disney Enterprises, Inc.

The Production Designer designs the movie. If necessary, he or she develops a visual style for the film, depending on the story, the target group and the budget. They translate the written script into visuals, including background- and character-styling, color and design language.

In the early stages of a new film, the Production Designer is part of the Visual Development team. This group explores all visual possibilities. They do research and try to come up with as many interesting ideas as possible, while working with complete artistic freedom. Usually at this time, the director is not yet involved.

As soon as a director has been assigned, the look of the movie is narrowed down. Some good directors have a vision about the look of the film and may be able to verbalize it.

Now the work of the visual development team is sorted out and a clear direction is defined. During this period of time, a production designer will be assigned to the project if he was not already part of the team.

The production designer now develops the final look of the movie in close connection with the director. Some presentation pieces showing the key moments of the story have to be done. They will reflect the look of the movie and backgrounds in combination with character designs. The preproduction team has to approve them before they are presented to the head of the production company for a final decision.

To sum it up to this critical point, in the beginning of a new production, a major part of the Production Designer's job is to sell the project with impressive-looking designs. That is especially important when outside investors are involved.

If no major disaster happens, the production is green lit. That means that the new project is announced to the outside world.

Now, it is necessary to analyze the style and to create a Style Guide. A style guide is a booklet of approximately 60 pages in which the basic rules of the styles are explained for the different departments: Layout, Background, Animation, Effects, Clean-up and Color. That is another very important step in the production process because so many different artists are involved. They have to learn everything about the new look and get used to it. For about the next eighteen months, they will have to live in that new world.

There is usually a training period of some weeks to allow the different artists to practice and create some test pieces. Sometimes new techniques have to be developed, especially for combinations of 2-D and 3-D. All of that is discussed in a smaller group of department heads together with the production designer, the art director and the director. During that time, sources for possible problems should be eliminated and the work pipeline refined.

During the same time, the production designer develops a precise color concept for the first sequence to go into production. Here it shows how important it is to create a Color Script for the whole movie at a very early stage, after the basic story is approved, because usually the first sequence in production is not sequence I; it can be from the middle of the movie.

Now that the train cannot be stopped anymore, the hungry crew has to be fed with everything they need. More sequences are approved one after another. It will be necessary to redesign certain changed locations. Props are always needed, little details such as the style for certain effects have to be developed. It all has to fit the look. And, of course, after the finished animation the production designer is part of the Sweat Box group to approve rough and final animation, as well as the color combinations.

Toward the end of the production, he is involved in the designs for publicity, the title logo, the posters, and the merchandise.

© Disney Enterprises, Inc.

ANALYS

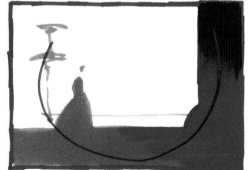

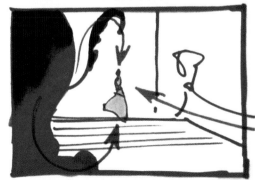

12

The scenes on the left from *Cinderella* show you how well-planned every single composition was. Note the Framing Effect and how all the background elements lead toward the characters. In addition, the action in every frame is clearly readable.

Look at the first scene where Cinderella enters the castle and seems to be lost within the huge architecture. You find her immediately; all the perspective lines lead you there.

In most of the other shots, you can find the same concept – big foreground elements frame the action; the characters are on a theatre stage in a pool of light.

The whole movie feels like a romantic theatre piece, like a Puccini Opera stage. Compare the simplicity of the designs to recent productions. Even with very few characters, they are able to tell a funny and very entertaining story. Joe Grant told me they did the whole movie in nine months! No wonder, after all the experience of the preceding masterpieces.

On the right, I have collected some more stunning compositions. There is no need to talk about the incredible style – *Mary Blair*. What else can I say?

..LEARNING

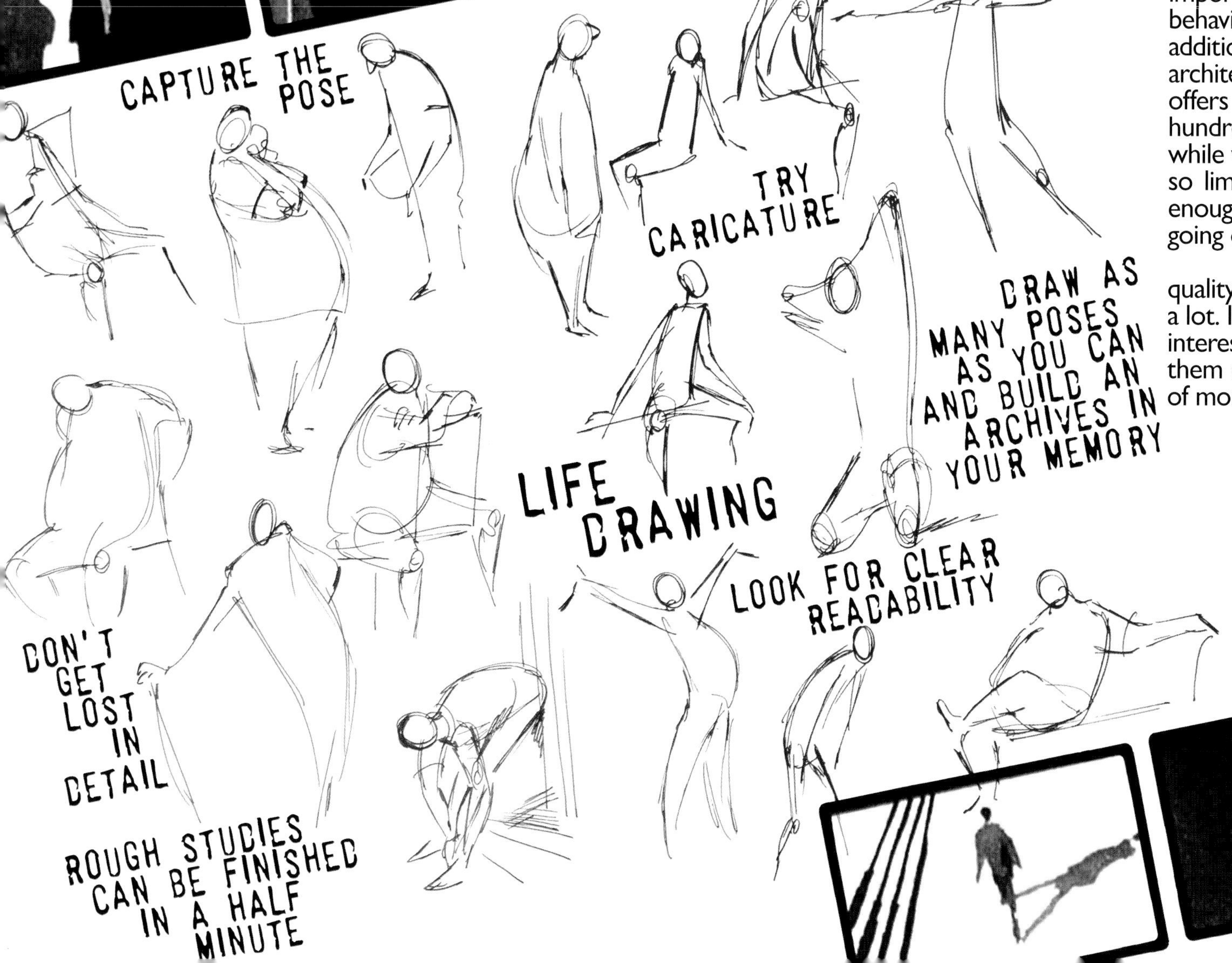

CAPTURE THE POSE

TRY CARICATURE

DRAW AS MANY POSES AS YOU CAN AND BUILD AN ARCHIVES IN YOUR MEMORY

LIFE DRAWING

LOOK FOR CLEAR READABILITY

DON'T GET LOST IN DETAIL

ROUGH STUDIES CAN BE FINISHED IN A HALF MINUTE

Sketching from real life is very useful. For a character designer it is important to watch people and their behavior; a production designer additionally studies the environment, architecture, styles and colors. TV offers a lot of these real-life images in hundreds of channels. I do sketches while watching TV. However, you are so limited because you are not fast enough and there is so much more going on.

During the early nineties, the quality of the video-printers improved a lot. I spent hours taping all different interesting programs to go through them afterward and print thousands of moments for reference.

In previous years, you were limited to creating your image archives by collecting magazines or doing your own reference photography. It was a very time-consuming job. Cutting out and sorting, took a lot of space and lots of boxes.

With the video prints all that improved. The Discovery Channel offered everything you ever needed for wildlife research, not to mention everything available on VHS, Laserdisc, and DVD.

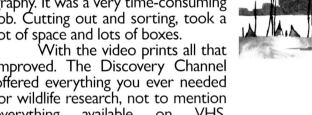

Well, over the years I have collected several thousand images in video prints. Very useful for all different assignments, but even more useful to get inspired. Just looking through the dozens of books with video prints gave me so many ideas.

It is even easier now, and cheaper. With available software, you create archives in your computer – no need for expensive prints. Moreover, it is then very easy to find what you are looking for with archiving software programs, not to mention that the picture quality is much better.

The choices are endless! Even without a background, just dealing with one character, you have a lot of choices about where to place the action. Does the story ask for a closer look at the face? Or do you need to be further away? On what side of the screen would it work? Closer to the edge, or more in the golden section? Do I choose an up-shot or a down-shot? A center-position usually looks boring, but would it work in this case? What do I want to say?

It gets a lot more interesting and challenging with two or more characters. What is the interaction? Do I need to show them up close, or does space between them characterize their relationship? Who is the dominant character? A size difference will make that clearer.

When you add background to your character-composition more choices come up. You can separate them by dark in front of light, or light in front of dark placement. So far we have not even added detail to our background, detail that has to be treated the same way as the action. I want to explain some examples of this visualization in the next chapters.

Most of my knowledge about composing and editing for film comes from watching and analyzing a lot of movies, commercials and music clips. After a while, you find out about the rules and understand why a film has been done a certain way visually and rhythmically to enable you to forget you are watching a movie. Bob Zemeckis, one of the great directors, said while I was working on *Roger Rabbit*, "We want the audience to forget they are sitting in a movie theatre, we want them to live in our movie." Maybe you've had that experience. If the music was an integral part of a film, you may not remember afterward that there was any music throughout the movie. Music helps to create emotions. To do the same with the visual part you have to understand a few things.

FILM

ANALYSIS

Choosing a good film to study helps one to find out about the rules. I am sure you can see the difference between just ordinary movies and the good ones. It has nothing to do with taste.

Following is a list of my personal top choices. You will notice that a lot of them are black & white films. Maybe you can concentrate better without being confused by colorful backgrounds, or maybe the better films are just black & white. But, there are some very good color movies out there as well. The problem with color is that it has to be designed as well. It's not enough to just go outside and shoot a movie.

Alfred Hitchcock – Rebecca, Spellbound, Paradine Case, Dial M For Murder, Vertigo, Psycho, The Birds, Frenzy

Andrzej Wajda – Ashes and Diamonds, Danton

Baz Luhrmann – Moulin Rouge

Bernardo Bertolucci – The Conformist, The Last Emperor, The Sheltering Sky

Bertrand Tavernier – Sunday In The Country, Beatrice And The Great 'Film Noir' Director

Billy Wilder – Double Indemnity, Sunset Boulevard, Witness for the Prosecution

Carl Reiner – Dead Men Don't Wear Plaid

Christoph Gans – Le Pacte Des Loups

David Lean – Oliver Twist, Bridge on the River Kwai, Dr. Zhivago, Lawrence of Arabia

Federico Fellini – La Strada, La Dolce Vita, 8 1/2, Satyricon, Amarcord

Franco Zeffirelli – Romeo and Juliet, Othello, Brother Sun, Sister Moon

François Girard – The Red Violin

Fritz Lang – Dr. Mabuse, Siegfried, Metropolis, M

George Cukor – My Fair Lady, Travels With My Aunt

Ingmar Bergman – The Seventh Seal, Wild Strawberries, The Silence, Winter's Light

Jacques Tati – Mr. Hulot's Holiday, Mon Oncle

Jacques Tourneur – Cat People, Out of the Past, Curse of the Demon

Joel Coen – Raising Arizona

John Boorman – Excalibur

John Frankenheimer – Grand Prix, 52 Pick-Up, French Connection

Ken Russell – The Music Lovers, Tommy

Michael Powell – Thief of Baghdad, Black Narcissus, Red Shoes, Tales of Hoffman

Michelangelo Antonioni – Blowup, L'Avventura

Mike van Diem – Character

Mikhail Kalatozov – The Cranes Are Flying

Milos Forman – Hair, Amadeus, Valmont

Norman Jewison – The Thomas Crown Affair

Orson Welles (My Personal Favorite) – Citizen Kane, The Stranger, Macbeth, Othello, Mr. Arkadin, Touch of Evil, The Trial

Peter Webber – Girl with a Pearl Earring

Peter Weir – Picnic at Hanging Rock, Year of Living Dangerously, Witness

Ridley Scott – The Duellists, Alien, Blade Runner, Legend, Black Rain, Gladiator

Roman Polanski – Repulsion, The Fearless Vampire Killers, Rosemary's Baby, Macbeth, Chinatown, The Ninth Gate

Sergei Eisenstein – Battleship Potemkin, Alexander Nevsky, Ivan the Terrible

Stanley Kubrick – Barry Lyndon

Steven Spielberg – Duel, Jaws, Raiders of the Lost Ark, Jurassic Park

Terry Gilliam – Time Bandits, Brazil, Twelve Monkeys

Vittorio De Sica – The Bicycle Thief, Miracle in Milan

Wachowski Brothers – Matrix Trilogy

Wong Kar-wai – In the Mood for Love

Woody Allen – Shadows and Fog

Zhang Yimou – House of Flying Daggers

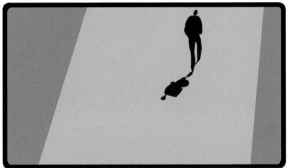 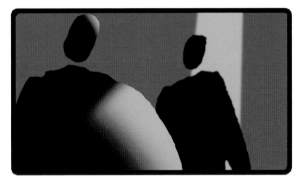 

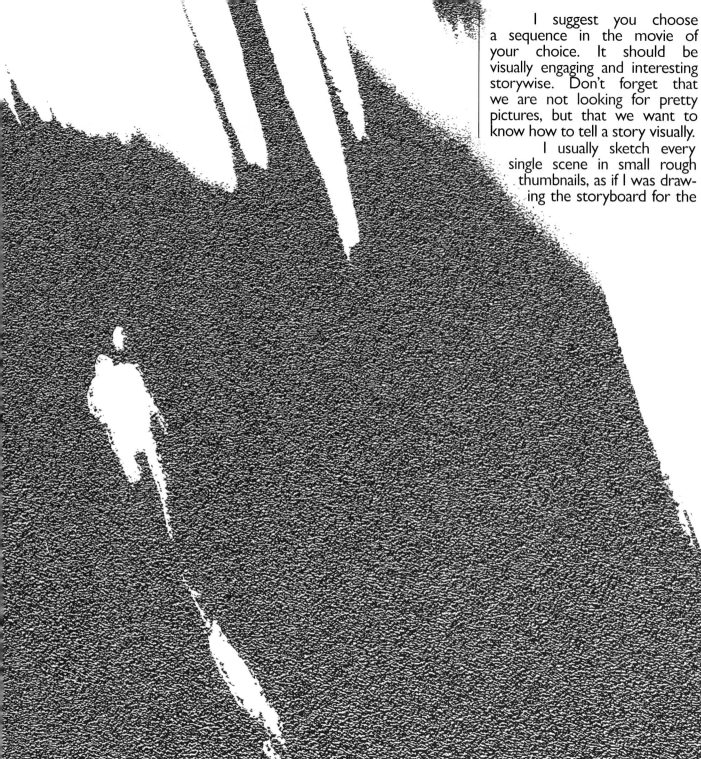

I suggest you choose a sequence in the movie of your choice. It should be visually engaging and interesting storywise. Don't forget that we are not looking for pretty pictures, but that we want to know how to tell a story visually.

I usually sketch every single scene in small rough thumbnails, as if I was drawing the storyboard for the movie. These boards are just the other way around as they illustrate a finished film. In case there is a moving camera or the actors are moving, you need to do several key drawings to indicate the most important steps.

Depending on the length of the sequence, you may come up with several hundred sketches. Prepared pages with small storyboard frames helps a lot.

Don't forget to use the correct image ratio. The oldest film format is just 3:4. Today, we have Wide-screen – 1:1.85, Cinemascope – 1:2, and Panavision – 1:2.35. The correct image ratio is very important; otherwise, you get different composition results.

The next step is preparing the floor plans for the different environments in your sequence. This step is very important. Try to analyze and draw the details of the scenes such as in an architectural sketch, the main light sources with arrows, the position of the characters and their movements, and so forth. Then indicate the positions and movement of the camera. You may need several pages with the same floor plan in case there are some complex moves.

23

You will learn a lot about different lens sizes, as well as how to cut from one shot to the next. Wide-angle lenses are used to establish a sequence or to cover some major character movement. Close-ups are done with the camera close to the actor or with telephoto lenses. You will see the difference; a telephoto lens keeps even distant objects or characters closer together with an out-of-focus effect. A closer wide-angle has a deeper depth of field with a bigger size difference. I will explain that in more detail in another chapter.

Always note: Why did they use that lens here with that size and how did they cut from one shot to the next? How did they connect the characters following the dialogue and the story?

Camera-angles: How was the camera positioned? At eye-level? Or is it an up-shot, or a cut to a down-shot? And why? In a horror-movie, you will find a lot of scary up-shots together with some effective use of light.

Always indicate in your floor plan where the light source is. You will notice that light and shadow in a row of shots is very important for your orientation. It is useful as well to study how projected shadows onto characters or objects are used to create depth and additional texture. Hitchcock apparently had the scenic designers paint shadows of furniture detail on the wall once in a while if they could not achieve that same effect with original light and shadow.

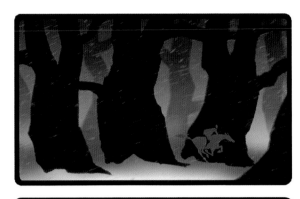

It is also interesting to analyze a moving camera. Antonioni is a master of that. Together with a very carefully choreographed move of his characters, he creates a voyeuristic effect; the audience is always in the center of the interaction between up to five actors.

We find a very different effect from that of a handheld camera in action sequences, together with a very fast editing and fast change of camera-angles.

Going through your thumbnails you can find out about composition rules, about the balance or un-balance in a shot, contrast and value, how the characters are staged and their integration in the environment.

The speed of editing creates a rhythm. Compare the length of different scenes. More emotional scenes have different lengths than action areas of a movie. Epic films such as *Lawrence of Arabia* have long establishing shots so that you feel the majestic power of the landscape images.

You will notice a lot of additional information in music-clips and commercials. Because of their restricted length and because they want to get all your attention within that short time, their rhythm- and composition-rules are different. And the images and their message are more important than a story. Often, you find crazy camera lens effects, manipulated colors, a shaky camera, grainy or ancient-looking film stock, as well as extremely fast cutting.

28

ONCE
UPON A TIME

The first *Beauty and the Beast* treatments were very serious. Well, it's a serious original story. There is nothing funny about a beast. I always compared it to *Snow White and the Seven Dwarfs* where you have the serious part with the witch and the dwarfs for comic relief. In *Beauty and the Beast*, we wanted to do it in a similar way, with the enchanted objects in the castle. But when I heard for the first time

that the plan was to change it into a musical, I was shocked. It's difficult for Europeans to understand how these ideas come up in the New World. We are very serious and would never even think about such an insult. I made jokes about a singing beast.

However, I was wrong. It worked. In addition, I must admit, I even like the music – which I cannot say about the look and some of the animation!

And, it started a new era in animation, with the following musicals: *Aladdin, The Lion King, The Hunchback Of Notre Dame, Pocahontas* and *Hercules*. Even in *Mulan* there is a lot of singing. And *Beauty and the Beast* was the beginning of the Golden Nineties in animation. I am happy I had a chance to be part of it.

In 1989, Disney started another London "adventure." Probably after the good experience with the European artists in London who worked on *Roger Rabbit*, Disney chose Dick and Jill Purdum as the directors for a new adaptation of *Beauty and the Beast*. Dick and Jill had an animation commercial studio in the West End. Their own work commitments did not allow them to leave London immediately to work on the project in Los Angeles, so they all decided to move some of the Disney artists for a few months to London to work on a story-reel of the project. There was Don Hahn, the producer; Andreas Deja and Glen Keane from animation; Tom Sito from story; Jean Gilmore from visual development; Derek Gogol from London, production design; Michael Dudoc du Witt, from storyboard; and me for storyboard and design.

31

We all worked in the Purdum studio during early fall of 1989. I will always keep these weeks in my memory as one of the best work experiences, to be in such a creative environment with all these high caliber artists and especially with Dick and Jill as the "parents" of the project, and Don Hahn with his unmatched humor.

We were all so committed that we worked 14 to 16 hours a day. At that time I remember that I did not see anything of London. We just worked like crazy. And we finished a story reel in color in a very short time, about 50 minutes long. The First Act: It was not a typical Disney movie, more a European version. But we all believed in it.

Well, they didn't in LA, and since they felt so bad to throw all our work in the trash, they decided to send us to the Loire area in France, where *Beauty and the Beast* could have happened in one of these beautiful castles. Our trip lasted 4 days, maybe 20 castles, and lots of driving, even more historic stories from "historian" Tom Sito, and so much fun. We were a family. That never happened again in my whole career. I felt so much at home. All the others did as well. We had good French food and even better wine. Of course nobody understood that some Germans liked sweetbread, horse steak and Bambi filet. From then on, they looked at me as the barbarian.

That reference trip could have created an incredible looking movie. We shot thousands of pictures, video, and did tons of sketches. Unfortunately, later in the movie it was decided not to use any of the reference and to do just another generic-looking Disney movie. Anyway, the

As you might notice, the very first designs I did for *Beauty and the Beast* very much shows the European influence. I wanted the village to look like a real medieval village. I always admired the architecture and look of the German silent movies *Der Golem* and *Faust* and some of the Siegfried forest scenes in *Die Nibelungen*. My approach was a bit influenced as well by movies that had just been released at the time: *Amadeus* and *Dangerous Liaisons*. And of course I used the painters of that time, Fragonard and Watteau, for inspiration.

SOME GRAPHS

	3	6	9	12	15	18
months

● rough treatment

story writing

production/character-design

environmental design

storyboard, addit./changes

sound recording

workbook + layout

background

character animation

secondary animation + clean-up

effects animation

character coloring

final editing/music

1. rough leica-reel
2. define leica-reel after sound rec.
3. exchange of elements in leica-reel rough anim/
   clean-up/colour

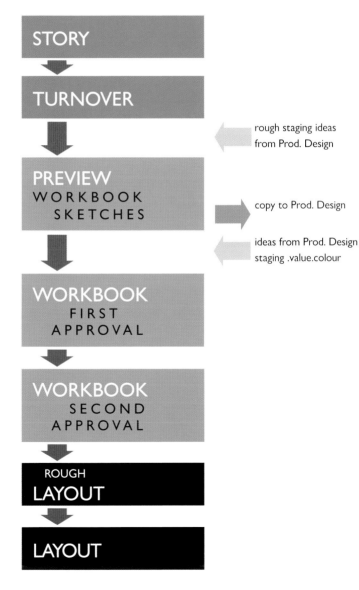

STORY

TURNOVER

rough staging ideas
from Prod. Design

PREVIEW
WORKBOOK
SKETCHES

copy to Prod. Design

ideas from Prod. Design
staging .value.colour

WORKBOOK
FIRST
APPROVAL

WORKBOOK
SECOND
APPROVAL

ROUGH
LAYOUT

LAYOUT

I am not a producer, so please don't take these graphs as the guidelines to produce an animated feature film. They are based on my experience through some productions and on talks with producers, especially Don Hahn.

Back in the late eighties when I was planning my own feature film, he gave me a crash-course, a four-hour lecture in producing an animated movie. I will never forget that Saturday morning. Afterwards, I had a headache for the whole weekend.

The only basic thing to understand is that everything on a film production happens overlapping in very carefully timed steps.

As you might have thought, the script comes first. But storyboarding goes on for a while. I even had experiences in which boards were still being redone during the last months of production. That is not a very economical way to work.

Checking my memories, I recall one production where we began animating somewhere in Act 2 because the opening was not yet finished. Not to mention not knowing how the whole thing would end! This is expensive because you might have to change or cut whole animated sequences when finally your story is complete, or, for example, when your hero is not a girl anymore, but a boy!

Another thing that can happen is that a small story detail that is very important for the ending has to be introduced in the beginning. Imagine if, late in production it is decided that the best idea to solve the ending is for the hero to use his or her "magic" sword. The sword has to be found during the first act and then carried visibly throughout the following sequences. Too bad it has to be added in that case into finished animated scenes. All that really happened – don't laugh. It is tragic!

There is a solution – start with a complete story! And don't change it. If a script is crap it should be finalized before you start to spend money. But I might think too logically. Maybe the real movies are done differently.

As for production time, I chose eighteen months because it always seemed to be the ideal length. The total length of time including preproduction can be much longer. I worked on *Mulan* for nearly five years. *Sleeping Beauty* took nine years to finish. On the other hand, Joe Grant told me that *Cinderella* was ready for release in nine months! Apparently, they knew pretty well what they needed to do. And they had an incredible experience at the time as a team.

Visual Development is the early stage in production where all the different ways to translate a story idea into visuals are being explored.

That includes the search for a style to fit the story, in all areas: background, characters, color, composition and editing. It also includes the research and concept-design based on possible stylistic directions.

Research into areas such as architecture, historical environment, landscape, costume and props starts simultaneously. Concept-design covers all different genres and styles, naturalistic or stylized, drama or romance, time-period movie, children or adult concepts, musical or action film.

The film-language has to be defined: Is it epic like a David Lean film, or character-driven like in an Ingmar Bergman movie, a thriller, possibly even black & white à la Hitchcock or a Chaplin situation comedy?

The visual approach is different in a thriller and in a comedy. Dramatic light and shadows, together with more

44

night-time scenes will dominate in a thriller or horror movie. A comedy is much lighter and colorful. Camera angles and editing will be very different as well. The more character-driven comedy has more close-ups with a normal camera, whereas an action movie uses more dramatic camera angles, up and down shots and very fast cutting.

Will the style of the film be realistic or abstract stylized, cartoony or surreal? How much detail can we afford to show without overloading the images? Do we lose the audience in an abstract visualization because it might be harder to establish an emotional connection to an abstract character?

The choice of color depends on the style and genre: fresh and friendly daylight colors for a comedy versus a dark mood and sharp contrasts in a thriller.

How big is the budget? Can we afford epic wide shots with tons of characters? On the other hand, do we have enough talent available for character-driven top-quality animation? Can stylized characters show the amount of emotion necessary to understand the story? How realistic can we go in the combination of environmental and character designs without getting trapped in a way too difficult and useless "un-cartoony" animation? All these questions have to be considered and discussed within the small team during that early stage of a new movie.

RESEARCH

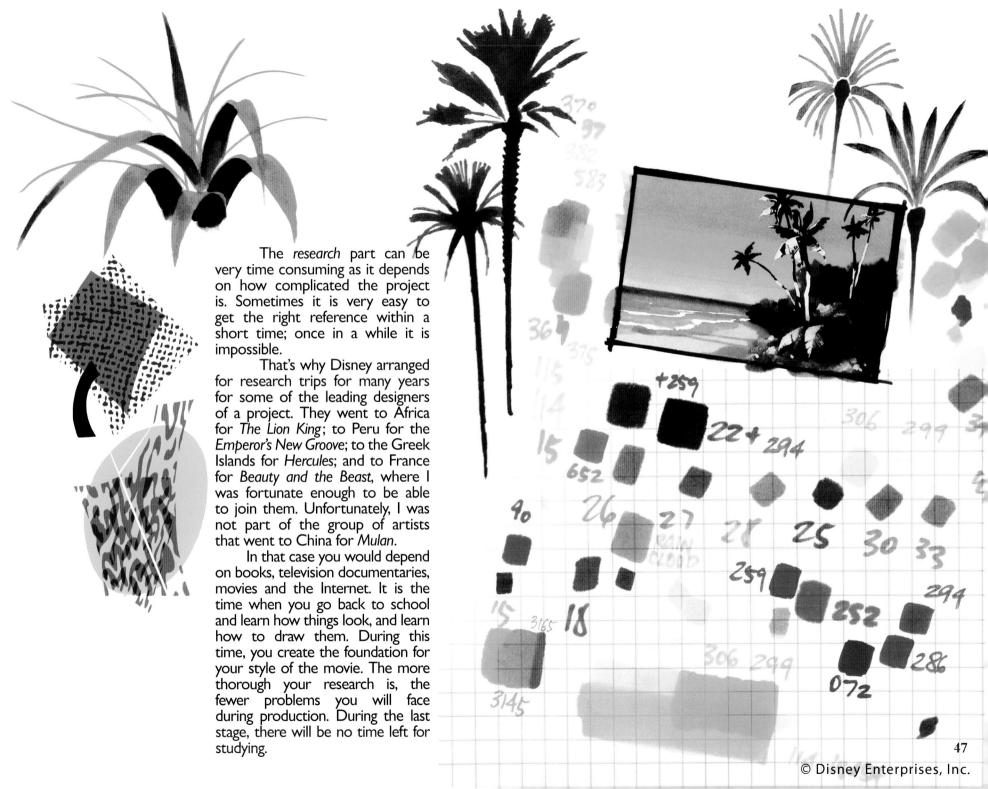

The *research* part can be very time consuming as it depends on how complicated the project is. Sometimes it is very easy to get the right reference within a short time; once in a while it is impossible.

That's why Disney arranged for research trips for many years for some of the leading designers of a project. They went to Africa for *The Lion King*; to Peru for the *Emperor's New Groove*; to the Greek Islands for *Hercules*; and to France for *Beauty and the Beast*, where I was fortunate enough to be able to join them. Unfortunately, I was not part of the group of artists that went to China for *Mulan*.

In that case you would depend on books, television documentaries, movies and the Internet. It is the time when you go back to school and learn how things look, and learn how to draw them. During this time, you create the foundation for your style of the movie. The more thorough your research is, the fewer problems you will face during production. During the last stage, there will be no time left for studying.

47

Aladdin

Working on *Aladdin* was a good experience. Ron Clements and John Musker wrote the script and directed the movie. Some musical numbers were written by the experienced team of *Beauty and the Beast*, Howard Ashman and Alan Menken. The story went through a lot of major changes. In the very beginning there were a few additional characters such as Aladdin's mother, but soon the story was streamlined.

The environment was that of *1001 Arabian Nights* and had to be designed well. There are a lot of movies that are set in that world, and we wanted to come up with something new. I found a lot of reference art books about the Orientalists, a group of mostly French painters around the end of the nineteenth century who concentrated on Middle Eastern themes. And I studied Persian miniature art for the palace garden. There were so many new art influences that I had never really cared about before. Among the Orientalist painters, I soon found my favorites: Jacques Majorelle and Jean-Leon Gerome.

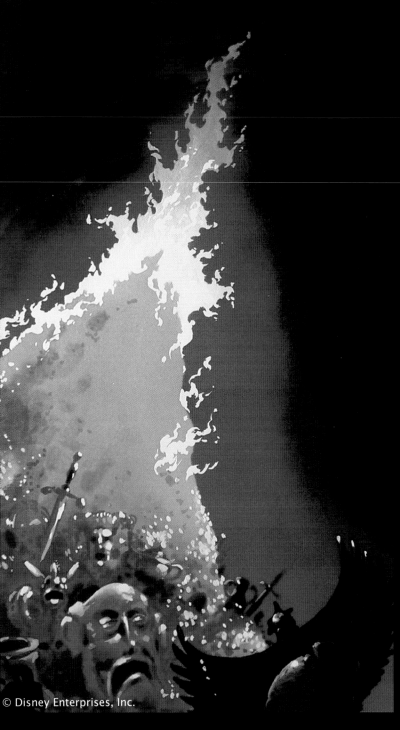

The style that Richard van der Wende, the assigned production designer, came up with was very interesting as well, a mixture of Orientalist paintings and the cartoony style that the studio used for *Peter and the Wolf* and some other shorts such as *Bongo* from the mid-forties. I came back to these shorts when I developed the style for *Mulan* several years later. So, it was a great learning time.

Then Eric Goldberg arrived. I had met Eric for the first time in 1977 in London when he worked for Richard Williams Animation. Later Eric had his own studio, Pizazz, in London. He decided to close it down and to move with his wife, Susan, to LA. As far as I remember, he had had enough of the business stress. Well, Eric took care of the genie, and he just cranked out hundreds of drawings in the shortest time. He was used to a different speed from his commercial days. And the genie he developed was amazing. We couldn't wait for the next animation tests.

Jippes, a comic creator, again in story-boarding. We had worked together on *Beauty and the Beast* and had become good friends. He was the storyboard genius. All of his boards could be framed and hung on the wall. What a

in London working on *Balto*, I convinced him to join us and he did the most amazing sequences. They influenced the animation completely. And we worked together again on *Mulan*.

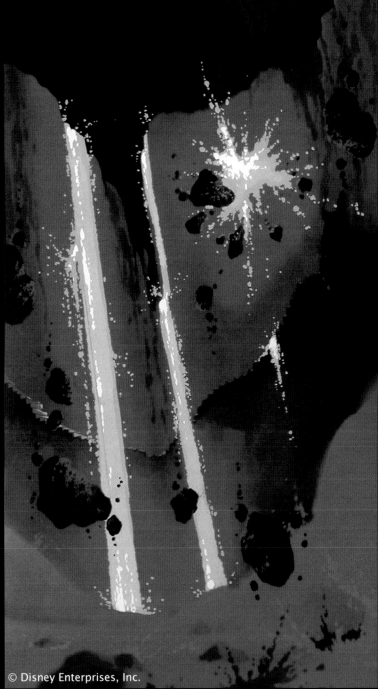

© Disney Enterprises, Inc.

Together, it was a very talented group of artists; not to forget Bill Perkins as art director; Kathy Altieri, head of background; and Rasoul Azadani, head of layout, and of course a little bit later when I was already working on *The Lion King*, Andreas Deja who animated Jaffar, one of the best characters in the movie, Mark Henn who animated the beautiful Jasmine, and Glen Keane with Aladdin.

© Disney Enterprises, Inc.

I got along with Richard van der Wende very well, and during the short time I worked on the movie I was able to design some interesting areas, such as the lion head in the desert, master sculpted for CG reference by sculptor Kent Melton. I was lucky enough to work with Kent for many years on a lot more movies. Then there was the whole cave sequence. It was fun to do the designs because I liked effects, and there were a lot of

them: exploding lava, fire and underwater. A bit later there was the treasure cave with all the collected treasures of the world: gold and jewelry. And I worked on the styling of the palace garden. That ended up very simplified in the final version.

Richard was a master painter. He had worked at ILM before and he had some matte-painting experience. Usually he painted the key backgrounds himself, very much as Eyvind Earle had done for *Sleeping Beauty*. That gave the

other painters a good example in which they could follow. When Richard was busy with one of his masterpieces, I had to fill the gap and design some of the missing areas. They were usually very fast felt-pen sketches. Once in a while I worked in pastel.

It was an incredible learning experience to work with all these artists. And I think it was the "masterclass" in the "Film Design School" that prepared me for the upcoming projects of the following years.

INSPIRATION

THE 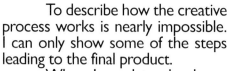CREATIVE PROCESS

To describe how the creative process works is nearly impossible. I can only show some of the steps leading to the final product.

When I need to develop a new style for a film, I want to come up with a look that nobody else has done before and that means that I should at least know what has been done. So far I have seen a lot of the animated movies from all over the world, and I have a big library of movies and books about animation from the past 70 years.

If time allows, I go through my archives and watch many movies done in different styles. I go through documentaries as well as selected comic books and art books. It may look like I just want to have fun looking at all that stuff. Yes, in a way it is fun, but more importantly, it refreshes the batteries! It's the best time, like going to school again. And it generates an energy that makes you want to create something.

What an experience to see how many beautiful things have been created. How diverse the world of art is, how differently all these artists from around the world see their world.

Imagine the variety: Australian Aboriginal art, ancient Indian temple sculptures, African tribal art, Albert Bierstadt's and Thomas Moran's majestic nature paintings, Ludwig Richter's and Gustave Dore's etchings, Picasso, Fragonard and Rembrandt, Steward Davis, Milton Glaser, A. J. Casson and Seymor Chwast, Moebius, Toppi, Franquin, Carlos Nine and Loisel. Not to forget Searle, McGinnis, Frazetta,

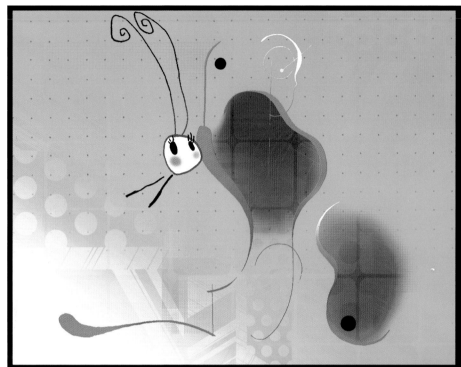

Rockwell and Oliphant, the Japanese woodcut masterpieces of Hokusai and Utamaro, animation designers like the Provensens, Jiri Trnka, Kay Nielsen and Tenggren, and so many more.

At one point I start sketching only little thumbnails, usually done with grey and black Japanese brush pens on paper. Of course, although all the art has had a big influence, somehow parts of all the things I am seeing are being mixed; perhaps a nearly abstract animal sketch from Eskimo art with the style of a Balinese silk painting. It's hard to explain what is happening at that time.

As a designer of a movie, you are not supposed to have a personal style unless a studio hires you because of it. Your job is to find and develop a look for a movie that works best with the story and does not feel like anything that has ever been done before. And it has to look good!

CAMERA RULES

In live-action movies, it is the cameraman who decides about the camera position and the picture size, and of course following the ideas of the director. In animation it is the layout artist who plans the use of the camera. He executes what has been planned in rough sketches in a *workbook* meeting. This stage is visually the most important moment of the movie, because at this point the storyboard is being translated into film language. Usually a storyboard in animation is not visually interesting. Its job is only to tell the story. The breakdown into different shots, perspectives, the choice of the number of characters in one scene, the exact location following a floor plan, the direction of the light, props, effects – all of this is decided in the workbook meeting. It is easy to imagine that only one sequence can be worked out in a several hours-long meeting, with all major department heads in attendance.

wide shot

side view profile shots

long shot

medium shot

close-up

shots are possible within a 180° radius from one side of the characters

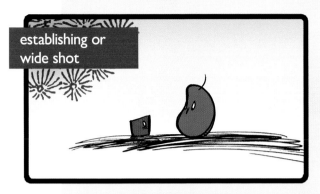

establishing or wide shot

A TYPICAL DIALOGUE SET UP

medium shot

master shot

close-ups

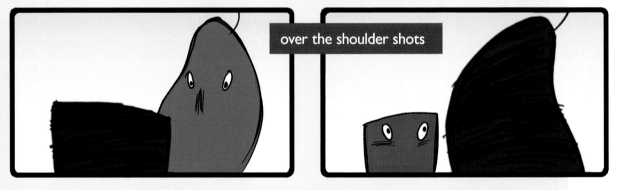

over the shoulder shots

Usually it is the job of the production designer to come up with sketches of the best choice of camera angle in these meetings. That's why it is so important to know everything about them, when to use them and why. It is not accidental to have a low positioned camera for an upshot. You want to emphasize a threatening situation, or during a dialogue

shoulder to shoulder

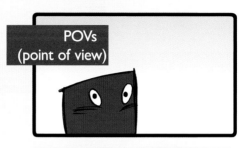

POVs
(point of view)

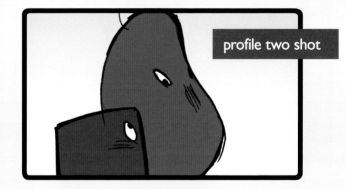

profile two shot

sequence explain the relation between characters. Dialogue scenes in particular need very careful planning. To make them interesting you cut from close ups to medium- or wide-shots, use over-the-shoulder or POV (point of view) positions. It gets more and more complicated the more characters are involved. You can confuse the audience completely when you jump around uncontrollably with your camera. The location and

eye level

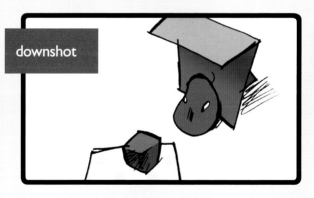

downshot

upshot

the relation of every single character to each other has to be followed by the movement of the camera. I will explain jump-cuts later. They can be a disaster and completely destroy a sequence. It is dangerous to lose control over a logical development of a sequence like that, and a confused audience will not be able to follow the story.

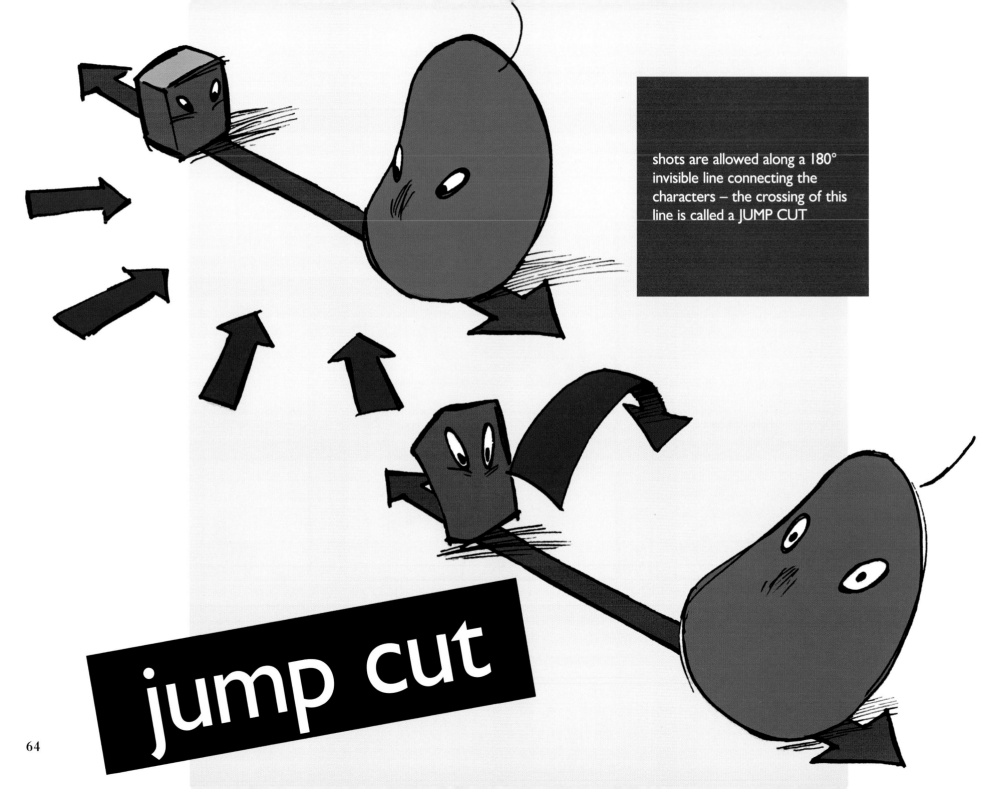

shots are allowed along a 180°
invisible line connecting the
characters – the crossing of this
line is called a JUMP CUT

jump cut

64

It is very helpful to work out the whole sequence in floor plans. The position of the camera and the movement from scene to scene is very easy to plan that way. The floor plan shows where the light comes from and what is important for the continuity during the sequence. You can even choreograph the movements of the characters that way before you translate everything into single cuts.

When movies are analyzed, it is very interesting to see and compare their visual rhythm, the number of wider shots compared to the close-ups, and within these shots the numbers of characters involved. This is very important for the budget of your movie. The more characters you have to animate, the more expensive your movie will be to make. Careful planning in the early stages will keep the costs down. It is not too difficult to work out a smart scene- and size-rhythm where you don't even notice that most of the time only one character is on the screen. Then you can spend your extra budget on establishing shots and action sequences with lots of characters in long- and wide-shots involved.

These close-ups or medium shots of one character need a very good animator though, because they have to show well-animated emotion, and lip-sync has to be accurate.

As you can see in these examples it is not too difficult, there are only a few rules you have to know. It is more important to be creative and to come up with new ideas for your own film language. But it doesn't hurt to study the masters and analyze why *Citizen Kane* looked so good.

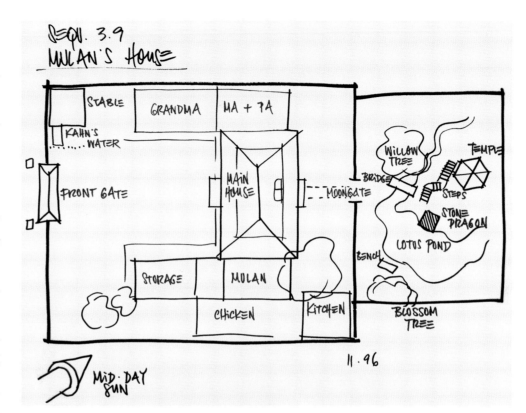

floorplans from MULAN

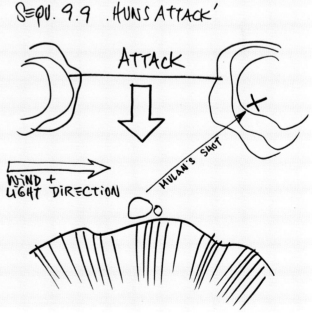

AFRICA

My adventure in Africa started in 1991, and the fairytale of Bambi in Africa was called at that time *King of the Jungle*. Had I known…

The first script pages I got were not very promising. Well, that had happened before. It makes it hard to start to work on a fresh project when nothing in the written version appeals to you. I was working from Germany. Nobody at Disney really believed in the project, so there was no budget to fly me to LA. That was very unusual as it had never happened before. George Scribner was the first director; later Roger Allers and Rob Minkoff took over. George wanted a very realistic look. He asked me to come up with visualizations of effects such as lens flare, out of focus to the extreme and more. The more crazy weather situations I could come up with, the better. As far as I remember I was one of the very first artists to work on that movie. It was not fun at all, because I was by myself and could not discuss the movie with the others involved. That's why I followed a call from Amblimation in London to work on *Cats* later that year.

Several years later I got connected again with the "*King*." It was short that time – overnight. That's how much time I had to come up with the logo for the Broadway show.

I had no idea how that would work on a theatre stage. When I finally saw the show at the New York premiere I was speechless. I liked the movie a lot, but the stage version is my favorite. Julie Taymor, the designer and director, is a genius. Everything worked with the music and I still get goose bumps!

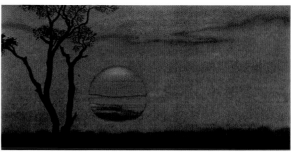

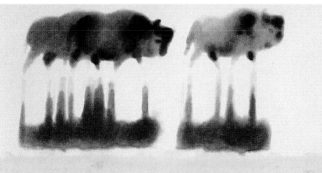

© Disney Enterprises, Inc.

Composition in film is the harmonious combination of shapes and movement within a field that creates an interesting imaginative world for the audience. We want the viewers to forget that it is a movie, an artificial world they are watching. A good story is the most important thing, but it has to be set in a believable world. And it has to fulfill visual dreams that are the same around the globe. The human brain has some basic understanding of the picture it sees, about the arrangement, the size and the balance in it. In film time it is limited. When you look at a painting you can take your time, get lost in the mood and the tiniest details. Our images are visible only for a few seconds, they have to be very precise in their arrangement. Nothing is accidental. We lead the eyes of the audience.

COMPO

OSITION

SOME BASIC RULES

camera angles and the length of the scenes. Action sequences are cut very fast, with scenes sometimes only a few frames long and with a very hectic change of close-ups and wider shots. Longer scenes and slower camera movements are used in slower-paced sequences.

The script, the mood and action in your scene as well as what has happened earlier and what will happen in the next scene will give you the keys for your composition.

Hectic and action-driven scenes are treated differently from peaceful, romantic scenes. It is amazing that a slightly tilted camera angle indicates that something disturbing might happen. This is made even stronger by the positioning of the characters, the use of light in front of dark or vice versa, and during the whole sequence a certain rhythm in editing. Everything has to work together. Composition and color of scenes in a sequence create what the script asks for. Pacing and storytelling is also determined by the cutting, and the very well-planned use of different

A good composition should have the right selection of *order*, *rhythm* and intelligent *balance*. That balance is between *space*, the negative area that is all around your objects and defines their shape, and the objects or the positive form that defines the readability of your design.

OBJECTS
positive shape

Find the *harmonious center* of your planned picture. Use it as the starting point for the placement of the action and all the necessary information around it.

Uninteresting placement of objects concentrated in one area should be avoided, as should placement on one straight line or precisely in the center of your field. You don't need to show each object at full length; you create more depth by cutting closer, moving them sideways and into the depth of your composition.

More importantly, lead the eye to the center of your "stage" where the action takes place.

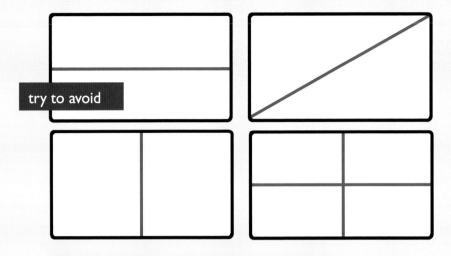

try to avoid

DISTRIBUTION OF SPACE

a better choice

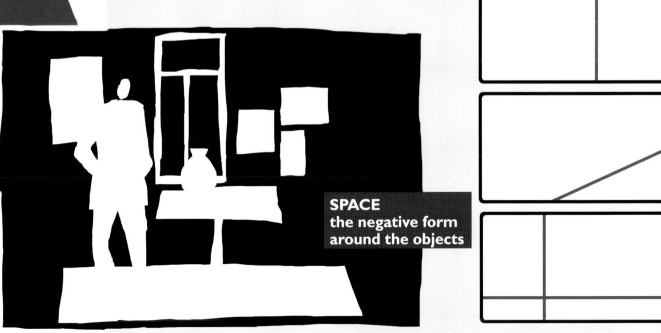

SPACE
the negative form around the objects

balanced composition

close-ups – cut off

open space

out of focus foreground

upshots – tilted camera

76

When I started work on *Brother Bear*, I collected a lot of ideas for image compositions. It became my personal guideline for visualizing a script. There always has to be a reason why you use a certain point of view; nothing is accidental. With the positioning of the camera, we do the first step of a statement. With lots of "air" around the action, we suggest freedom of movement, wide open space – peace. The movement of the character within our frame can say a lot about the mood or the situation. A balanced composition with the main action in the center, or golden section, will indicate a balanced feeling. And all that is only about the distribution of important elements within our picture, and not about color. That's why I chose only simple black & white roughs. Color will enhance your basic composition in a later step.

The format is a very important factor. In a normal 3:4 format from the old days, the positioning of characters is very different compared to a Cinemascope or

Panavision format. Deciding where to cut to a close-up in these wide formats can be especially tricky. A close-up of a face that is not close enough leaves too much empty space around it. These extreme close-ups were a big problem in the days when the animation still had to be painted on cells. Very often the big empty color areas in between the few lines of a face had their own "animated" life, the color was usually not evenly applied and the image flickered.

Movement within the frame has to be designed very differently in a wide format as well. The camera is panning much more often in a normal 3:4 format, as soon as a character starts to move, the camera has to follow. In the wider formats, the action has more room within the bigger field. But it is difficult here as well to plan the character- and camera-movement. It is following different rules. A too hectic camera movement within a picture that big creates a lot of nervous tension where we don't really need it. Another big difference is *when* the camera starts to move. Usually the character movement initiates the moving of the camera as the camera always "follows." In a normal format, there is not that much room for a character to move, so the camera will follow pretty much at the same time. In wider formats, we can give the character a lot more room along with a more gentle treatment of the camera. And it is easier in these wide formats to really compose a picture, balancing positive and negative space as well as the action.

interesting moving patterns

size difference + out of focus

underwater + distortion effect

interesting cutting – extreme close ups…

…to extreme wide

77

© Disney Enterprises, Inc.

diagonals – shadows/snowpatches/ rockshapes

positive/negative

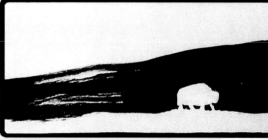

"breaking the rule"

different levels – depth

organized chaos

An animated film is a succession of static images that comes to life. Norman McLaren said, "Animation is not the art of drawings that move, but the art of movements that are drawn."

We have to think about the later result, the moving image, in our planning stage. It is the visual concept that creates a movie, and the rhythm of these visuals creates an interesting film.

Hundreds of the most beautiful close-ups, one after another, don't make a good movie. A good film consists of well-planned composition of very differently staged shots, like the ones in thumbnail sketches in this chapter.

There are visuals that create peaceful emotions. The background composition is balanced. Aggressive moments will show hectic designs and a chaotic and unbalanced composition. Usually the climax of a movie is built by images that create tension. Tilted camera angles, harsh contrasts in light and shadow, a well-planned rhythm of close-ups and wider shots, as well as a disturbing composition of background details lead us there.

downshots –
shadows reveal shapes

framing within the
frame

moving in + out of
shadow, clear read-
ability

unusual compositions +
effects

different moving speed
depth

79

© Disney Enterprises, Inc.

**rhythm/
graphic abstraction**

softness

dimensions

**changing horizons
epic compositions**

80

What is it that makes an image? First of all, there is the action, the movement. It is what separates our movie image from a "still" image.

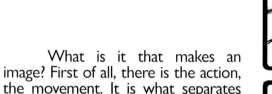

The movement can be that of an object or a character: the hands, face or the whole body. The camera can follow the movements, or the camera can move independently from the character. Among the "horizontal" movements (pans), camera moves from left to right are more accepted. It is our writing and reading direction. Knowing this, the opposite move from right to left can be used more dramatically.

"Vertical" camera moves follow an object up into the air or the other way around. Then we have "diagonal" moves, and also moves into or out of the picture (truck in/out).

Very rare are circular moves around a character or object, such as in *Snow White and the Seven Dwarfs* in the scene with the queen drinking the magic potion. In that case, background and foreground are moved in opposite directions and the character is animated correspondingly.

depth

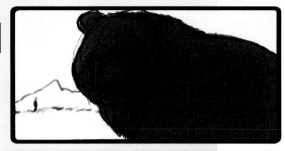

tilted angles – dramatic composition

interesting framing – proportional dark + light

dramatic up ...

... down shots

In the background behind our character, we have to deal with several different items: *linear elements*, *shapes* and *values*.

Lines are everywhere, straight and curved, pure lines or lines as part of an object. They have to be treated very carefully, because they can indicate a separation or direction. Tangents must be avoided as well as lines leading the eye into the corners of the image. Parallel lines are dangerous unless they are wanted for design reasons, as are the lines dividing the images into equal parts. A part of the style of *Mulan* was to avoid straight lines. Sloppier (controlled sloppy) drawn lines look cartoony, while precisely straight lines belong in an architectural design.

The *shape* is the definition of objects in the background, such as architecture, trees or mountains. We usually arrange overlapping shapes in our composition. It is important to create interesting-looking shapes, which leads us to *values*. Values define our shapes and their position within the background. During the planning of a scene, we usually work with four to five grey values. They separate the design into the positive and the negative shape, as well as the mid-range values. There will be more about this in a later chapter.

In a planned value scheme, a silhouette can be light in front of dark. All the different elements of our image have to be clearly readable. The design's composition has to work well within a continuous arrangement of scenes. It has to fit into the puzzle, a piece within a sequence, and several sequences within the movie.

interesting
dividing of space

size exaggeration

open space

beauty of nature

83

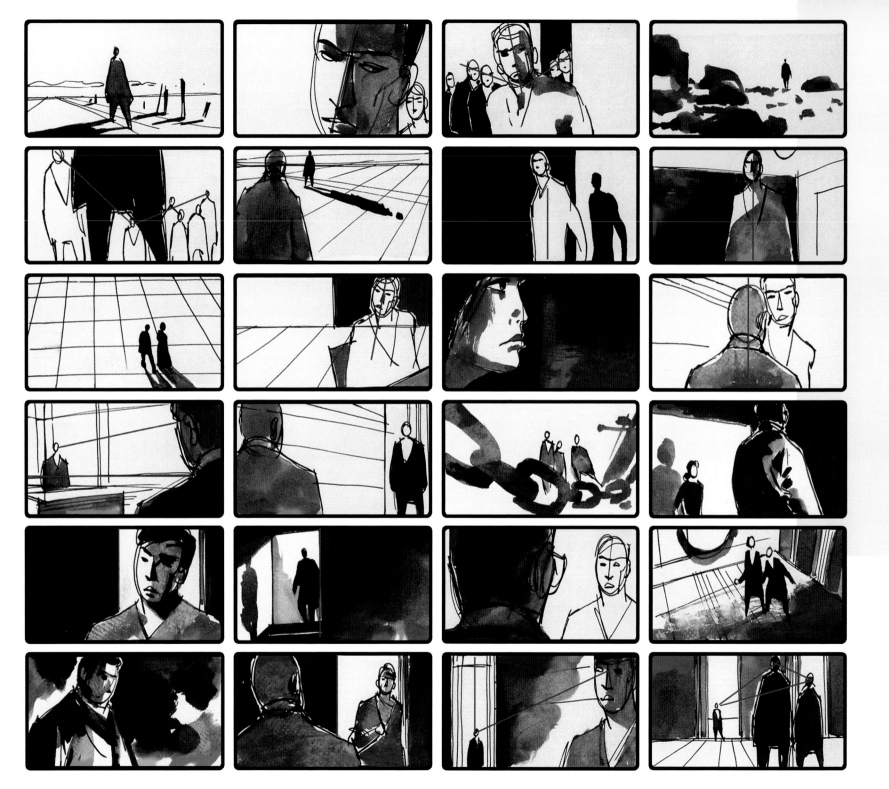

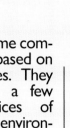

Here are some composition studies based on live-action movies. They show you only a few interesting choices of character and environment combinations within a wide-screen format.

The interaction of characters is always interesting, as is their placement in relation to each other. The characters provide the most interesting way of moving the different puzzle pieces around.

The ingredients and their variation are the key: the depth within your field, created by a combination of foreground and background, use of light and dark contrasts and different focus levels. Then the arrangement of the characters to each

other (in case you have more than one). Use the *triangle* rule to avoid the uninteresting succession of figures that appear the same size right next to each other. And go for *simplicity*! I try to avoid detail wherever possible. In our design-planning stage, detail should only be added where it is needed to explain the story. It is interesting to note that if your sketch works without the detailed stuff, the final background should do it as well. I am not talking about texture. When used correctly, texture creates a tone. Flat color areas without a certain amount of texture can be part of a style, but usually the information that texture gives us is necessary to describe materials and creates depth.

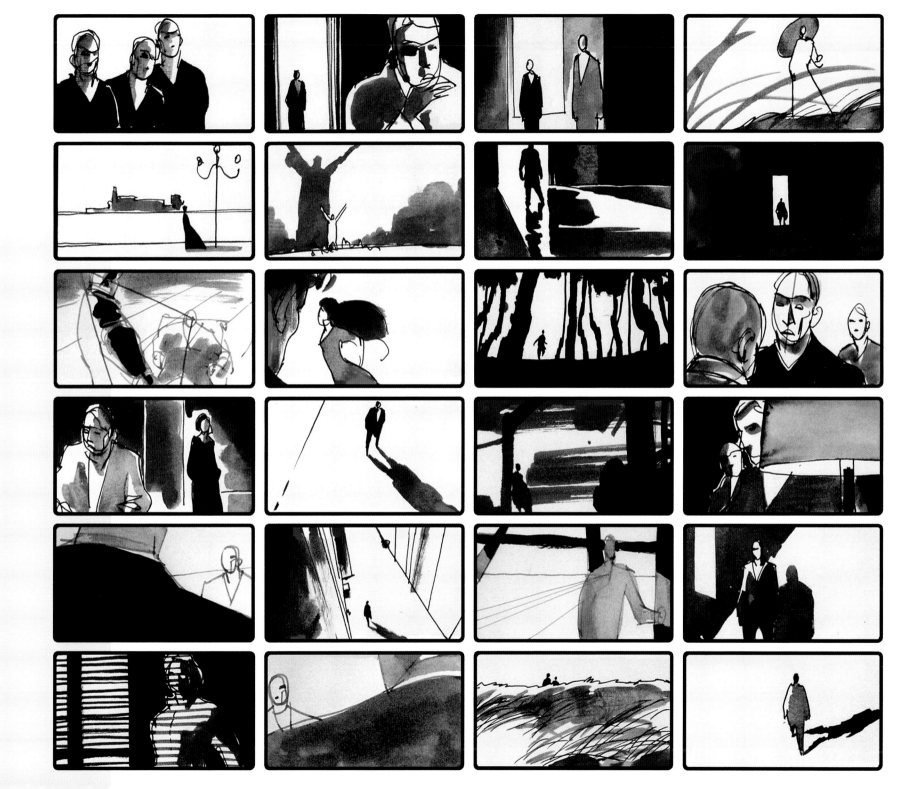

OLYMPUS

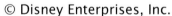

I worked in preproduction on *Hercules* for about six months. John Musker and Ron Clements were the directors. We had worked together on *Aladdin*. Andy Gaskill was the assigned art director. My job was to develop a few style ideas over a short term. Andy and I did a complete color-script together. He created all the incredible thumbnails like a miniature storyboard within a very short time. Most of them were drawn right on the script pages. I loved his work.

89

From every page, I selected some sketches as keys and colored them. That's how the color script was finally developed. Afterward, I developed an abstract color continuity script. It was fun to work on something so different from all the previous movies I had been involved in. Nothing in that script was serious; it was pure sitcom.

© Disney Enterprises, Inc.

vases influenced the characters in the movie. In general there were a lot of very challenging environments, like Hades (the underworld) and Olympus, residence of the Greek gods.

© Disney Enterprises, Inc.

It was not one of my favorites as there was too much talking, but there were some great characters like Hades.

To design some of that environment was interesting as well. The old classic Greek world was not taken seriously at all. We studied a lot of antique vases. Even the way humans were drawn on the

© Disney Enterprises, Inc.

Some amazing freelance artists were involved, such as Bruce Zick, Gay Lawrence, and Valerio Ventura. A lot of their work influenced the final look of the movie.

Shortly before I left to work exclusively on *Mulan*, Gerald Scarfe joined the team and took over the designing of the characters and in part the look of the movie.

STAGING

Staging is the placement of the characters within a set. The characters have to be part of the composition of the whole image and their placement in relation to each other has to work. If the characters are moving, a choreographed movement has to be planned. For dialogue scenes, precise camera angles and cuts have to be prepared and the direction of the light and corresponding shadows defined in floor plans.

All this is not the sole responsibility of the production designer; the director also decides about these issues, but you have to come up with ideas and you have to know about all the technical details.

It is very important to create a rhythm in your compositions. Some directors in live-action movies have even developed a distinctive style in the way their movies are cut. But, first of all, you have to visualize the story. Then you start to refine your images.

It doesn't make sense to use the most stunning visuals and have the most interesting camera angles, as well as staging and movement of the characters when it has nothing to do with the story. Music videos can afford to do that since they want to keep your attention for four minutes, and they can go over the top with their effects. Advertising commercials are similar, but you should not do that in a feature film. It is like too much sweet cake with whipped cream. You begin to feel sick after a while.

It is also important not to give everything away within the first part of the movie. You want to keep something special for the climax of the film, the most incredible combination of camera angles, movement and color. Start slow, take your time to establish the mood, and then accelerate with the speed of the story toward the climax. Staging here can be crazy, cuts very fast, and colors unusual. And slow down to the end.

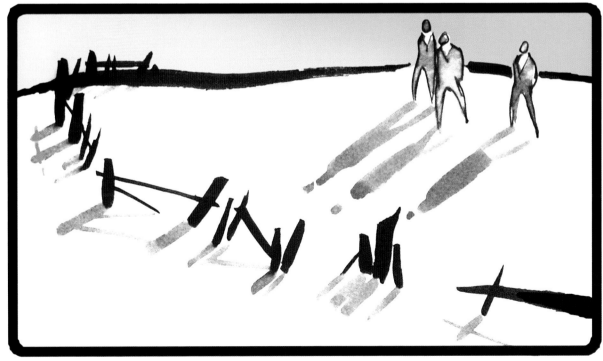

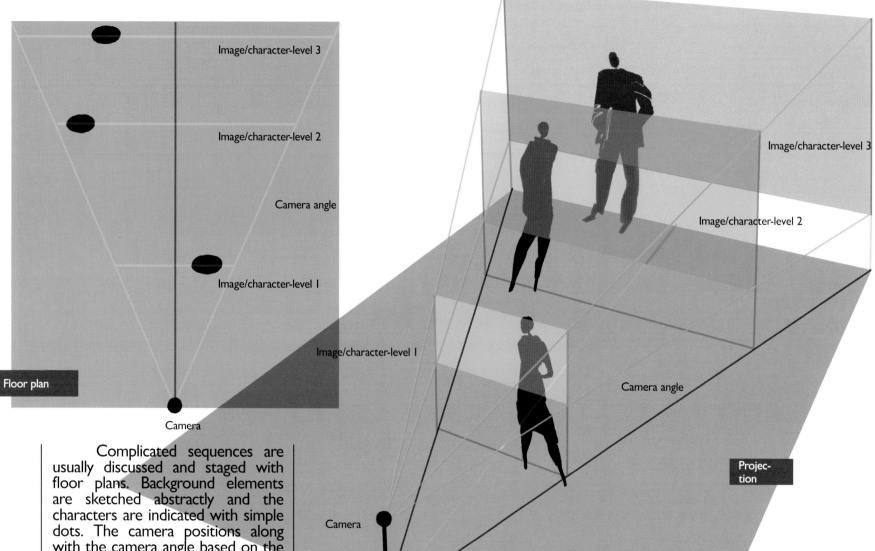

Floor plan

Image/character-level 3

Image/character-level 2

Camera angle

Image/character-level 1

Camera

Image/character-level 3

Image/character-level 2

Image/character-level 1

Camera angle

Projec-
tion

Camera

Complicated sequences are usually discussed and staged with floor plans. Background elements are sketched abstractly and the characters are indicated with simple dots. The camera positions along with the camera angle based on the camera field are sketched in as well.

That way it is possible to plan the necessary character-moves together with the corresponding camera positions and moves. What the dots and angles don't show, is if all combinations of characters in their different sizes together with the background will be good-looking and interesting compositions.

Of course you can sketch a rough interpretation of a floor plan situation the way the camera would see it. To be sure to find possibly better staging you can use the *projection method*.

It is a simple translation of a floor plan with actor positions and camera angle into a three-quarter perspective view. You can follow the different steps in the samples on this double-page illustration. It is not the very complex projection method that film architects use. I tried that system once while working on a live-action film and found it very complicated.

94

Level-sizes

As you can see in the final combination of the three character-levels, the composition in this case works pretty well. If you are not happy, just shift the position of the characters in your three-quarter view until you are satisfied.

If you have down- or up-shots, the construction in your projection sketch will be a bit more complicated. But I only use this method for very carefully planned positioning of the action and the camera. An even simpler method is indicated on the following page.

Image through camera

To be a bit faster with acceptable results for animation, I developed this simplified version for myself. Today, working with the computer is even faster and more accurate. I know there is 3-D software on the market that will do an even better job, but I never left the 2-D stage.

Every layout artist knows this method. You have two or more related characters involved in a scene. Some of them are seen to be closer shots where you don't see the characters' contact to the ground level. If you think you can just make it up, that never really works. The problem is the perspective. The characters with and without visible ground-contact have to follow the same perspective grid.

The solution is pretty simple. You know the horizon-level in your design. Place your foreground character in the same size relation next to the background character. Following the perspective grid, it is fairly simple to find the later invisible ground contact for your foreground action.

These are some simplified visuals to show you the different results using different lens-sizes.

As you probably know from photography, the smaller the lens-millimeter size, the wider your picture; the bigger the millimeter size, the closer you can go into the far distance. Lenses from about 20mm to 35mm are *wide-angle* lenses. Everything closer to 50mm is a *normal* lens. From about 150mm upward, we call them *telephoto* lenses.

It is not only the different amount of information you get with these lenses, the motifs have a very specific look. Wide-angle lenses show a lot of perspective, especially when you use them combined with up- or down-shots. They have a funny effect on portraits when used for close-ups. Normal-lenses are similar to what our eyes see, perspective is not too exaggerated, and the focus level has to be precisely chosen. Extreme foregrounds will be out of focus. The effect you get from telephoto lenses is very interesting. They seem to eliminate perspective; you will find a lot more parallel lines. And everything except your focus level will be out of focus. Objects in the far distance seem to be closer to each other than they really are.

In animation we don't actually use different camera lenses. We draw what their result would look like. From the experience of the different looks you get with a variety of lenses, you can create very interesting visuals. A composition of three related characters will look very different if you design it with either a wide-angle or a telephoto look. You have another design element in your toolbox, an element that will improve your visual language.

24mm Wide-angle lens

50mm Normal lens

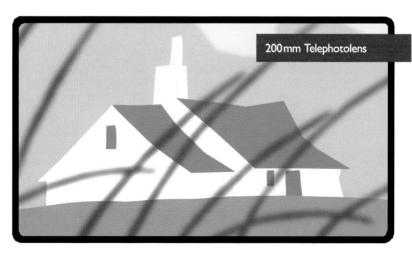

200mm Telephotolens

FORMATS

normal format 3 : 4   widescreen 1 : 1.85   cinemascope 1 : 2   panavision 1 : 2.35

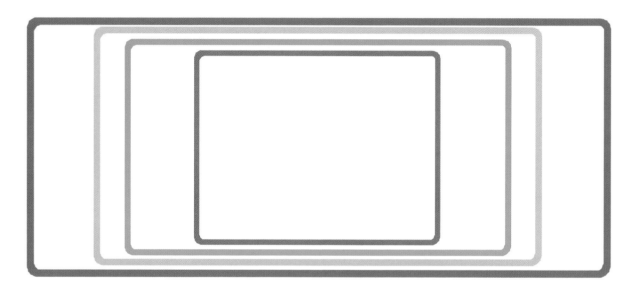

Edison and Eastman Kodak were the first to produce 35mm film at the end of the nineteenth century. This 35mm celluloid stripe had perforation holes on both sides to transport it through the camera. The area in between was 1 inch or 2.54cm wide. That defined the width of the exposed picture, its height was the distance measured between 4 perforation holes, or 3/4 of an inch, or 1.9cm. That's why it is called *3:4 format*. In the old days, one foot of film contained 16 frames, running at 16 frames per second through the camera.

Later, different formats were invented such as Cinemascope. It used the same 35mm film format but squeezed the picture using an anamorphic lens. The projected un-squeezed format was an impressive 1:2. Very common today is a slightly smaller 1:1.85 format, called *widescreen*.

And there are the super-widescreen formats such as ToddAO and 70mm, with the 1:2.35 dimensions. It is widely called Panavision format.

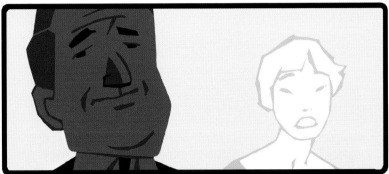

As you can see on the left, the different formats create their own rules for composition and camera-moves.

In close-up shots, it is easy to place the character into your normal format frame. To keep the same amount of negative space around the face in a super-widescreen format, you have to cut off a lot more around the face. If you don't, it will not be a close-up anymore and you will have too much empty space around the face.

Composing with two or more characters, on the other hand, is much easier in the wider format and you have a lot more choices for a good composition. But there is so much room for information in this big image that you have to be very careful how much you use without overloading it.

The way you move your camera in these formats is very different. With a moving object you have to start your camera-move very early so as not to lose the action. In a wider format, there is a lot of room around the moving objects or characters. You let the character move halfway through your picture and then start speeding up your moving camera. For most moves in a wider composition, it is not necessary to move the camera at all, but it makes it more challenging to arrange the right choreography of your action.

The same rule applies to panoramic shots. To show that majestic wide landscape in a normal format you would either go much wider, which increases the amount of sky, or you would need to move your camera.

99

My *Mulan* story begins in September 1993. At that time, I was still working in London at Spielberg's Amblimation studio. I was production designer/art director on *Balto*. Andreas Deja, a good friend and former student in Germany, now one of the top animators at Disney, had called me and talked about a future project they were planning: *China Doll*. He explained the showdown between the emperor, Mulan, and her army friend. I liked that ending actually way more than the ending in the final film. It was a mix-up story, where Mulan had to decide between the life of the emperor and her friend Shang. Anyway, that story sounded too good and it was set in China! What an opportunity for designs in a very new style, mysterious, poetic, and exotic. And I was stuck in London in that icy Alaska movie. Well, I bought some books about Chinese art, because I had no idea about that part of the world and their culture. The more I read and the more I saw, the more I got trapped!

I started to do some sketches, just for myself and without Disney knowing about it. Funny thing is, Barry Cook, the first *Mulan* director, saw these designs later and they made him decide that I was his first choice to design the entire film.

Well, in March 1994, I left London and the Amblimation crew. *Mulan* was not the reason. It was the very uncertain future of that studio. Nobody wanted to tell me any details of Spielberg's plans. About a year later, I understood

why – he started DreamWorks together with Jeffrey Katzenberg and David Geffen in Los Angeles. And most of the artists I had worked with in London moved to LA and worked "next door."

I moved with my wife Hanne in June 1994 to LA and started to work at Disney, the first time in my life I was employed there. A new experience! My first projects as visual development artist were *Hercules*, *Fantasia 2000*, *The Steadfast Tin Soldier*, Beethoven's *Symphony No. 5*, and *Dinosaur*. *Mulan* already had a development crew that had been working on it for nearly one year. Among them was Chen-Yi Chang, who later became the character designer of the movie and my good friend. I could not have designed *Mulan* without him. He very patiently explained everything about China, gave me the real books and background information – and he knew the best Chinese restaurants in town!

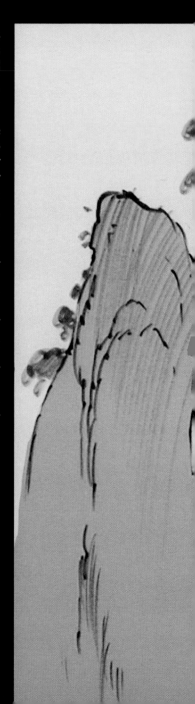

© Disney Enterprises, Inc.

The *Mulan* visual development team had problems with the style. They tried to copy Chinese water-color paintings, but did it the Disney way, with tons of detail everywhere and were kind of lost. Barry Cook, the director, asked me in December, 1994 to take over as production designer. That was a challenge. I had no clear idea where to go, but I knew I didn't want it to look like the recent Disney movies, for example, *Beauty and the Beast, Aladdin* and *The Lion King*. My dream was to create a look that was more similar to my favorite older masterpieces.

Chen-Yi had shown me some original Chinese comic books. Each about 300 pages thick, with very delicate black & white drawings in some styles I had never seen before. They showed a very unique way to draw trees, mountains and villages. Not to mention the human characters, animals and props.

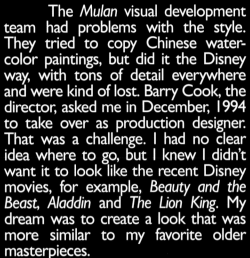

They were fascinating. In a way they completely changed my design thinking. Then I noticed that in most of the separate hundred-year-old watercolors, there was something that made them very typical. It took weeks until I finally understood. It was the lack of perspective and fine detail. It made them look very flat.

I immediately started to use that experience in my own designs. Their size was very small and that is what helped. The bigger you draw or paint the more detail you want to add. Because of the small thumb-nail size of my color sketches I did not even think about that. Later during the production, I asked the background painters to throw all brushes below size four away. Detail was not allowed.

These preproduction years 1994–1996 were incredible! When you are used to working in the advertising or TV-world you are not used to the luxury of having all that time, time to search for something, though you don't quite know what it is. It's a luxury only a few studios can afford. And it might only have worked in those years because it was the 'Golden Nineties' in animation after all those successful hits.

The studio gave me the chance to invite 'guest-artists' from all over the world. We wanted to explore all different talents to add more ingredients for a unique look for our movie. Among these artists were – Alex Nino, a comic legend from the good Marvel days. Born in the Philippines, and living in LA – what an artist! I still don't understand how he works. He starts in one corner of a large A2 paper and finishes it in the afternoon with the most incredible scenery showing action and mood and without one rough sketch line. It's all in his head. Then, Regis Loisel, best known

for his comic adaptation of *Peter Pan* has a completely different style. What an artist, again! I felt so honored to have had a chance to work with them and to have fun together. Others were Vink, a Belgian/Vietnamese comic artist and Harald Siepermann, my comic strip partner of the A. J. Kwak series and former student. All those artists contributed their view to a growing huge package, a collection of *Mulan* ideas.

There must be thousands and thousands of sketches in the Disney archives from that time. Every single sketch was discussed together with the two directors: Barry Cook and Tony Bancroft. We decided together what we should use and what was going in a too different art direction.

112

At the same time, I was diving into the world of art. I had never done that before, because there was never enough time. Job delivery next day! Now I found out about all these artists of the past, completely unknown to me, not through books, but through auction catalogs from Sotheby's and Christie's. I also found them used and inexpensive in the numerous LA flea markets on the weekends. After some years, I had collected 1,500 of them; I specialized in Chinese art of course, in Impressionists, nineteenth century and modern art. After a while, I selected a few from the thousands of art pieces that I thought I could use as inspiration for our movie.

There was Jean-Baptiste-Camille Corot, a French painter from the Barbizon school during the eighteenth century. Beautiful washes in oil, no detail at all — mood! mood!! — more like matte paintings for a movie. From a distance they made sense. There were some more, such as Franz Richard Unterberger; who worked in Belgium during the Nineteenth century;

Eugene Galien-Laloue, who worked during the same period, with his precise architectural paintings of Paris; and, opposite Giovanni Boldini, an Italian painter with his rough expressive style. And of course all that Chinese art from the last four centuries. Including calligraphy — beautiful. I learned about the

philosophy, the Yin and Yang, the balance everywhere that influenced all those amazing landscape washes with detail in some areas, but more like texture, and more and more detail toward the foreground in the very stylized blossoms, bamboo and grass. Exactly what I wanted to see in the movie.

But I knew that too much art would destroy the acceptance by the audience. An audience wants to be entertained, not educated. So, what we had to come up with was the feel of China embedded in a commercial Disney movie.

Somehow we had to find a way to make the movie look like a Disney movie. Not like *The Little Mermaid*, *Beauty and the Beast* or *Hercules*. More like the masterpieces of the old days like *Bambi* and *Pinocchio*, even the *Silly Symphonies*. The Walt Disney Archives contains the "Animation Research Library," and Lella Smith and her crew were especially a big help going through many original backgrounds and layouts of these milestones in animation.

It's hard to explain how you feel when you hold one original background from Pinocchio, painted such a long time ago, in your hands. We were nearly whispering like you would in a church. Those guys back in the Forties did not know what they had created: the water-color backgrounds of the *Silly Symphonies*, *Pinocchio*, *Dumbo*, *Fantasia* and a lot of the others, and the oil painted forest scenes of *Bambi*. There was no unnecessary detail. They were pure empty stages for the action to follow.

I still get goose bumps when I remember the beautiful layouts in *Bambi*, graphite paintings, masterpieces; everything was right, the composition, the mood, the translation of reality. That's what we needed. But nobody was there to teach us. The only way was to analyze the old work on *Bambi*, *Pinocchio* and especially *Farmyard Symphony* (Disney *Silly Symphonies*), and to try to use these golden rules for our movie. That's how my *Style Guide* for *Mulan* started.

Ric Sluiter, who was assigned as art director, was working very closely with me. He is a master painter in all techniques: Watercolor, oil and gouache. And he explained to me how these guys had painted. The secrets! I was called during the London time "the magic marker

wizard." That was the technique I had used for years. It was fast, dirty and dangerous. But the final artwork looked very close to a printed piece of art and the colors were vibrant. I was pretty good in all the different ways to fake a watercolor look. That's how I had done all the hundreds of designs for *Beauty and the Beast, Aladdin*, and *Hercules* and now for *Mulan*. But I realized I needed to paint big, in the original painting style, in gouache. I needed to show what I thought the backgrounds should look like in a technique everybody could follow.

The little thumbnails I had done always looked a bit out of focus. That effect was very hard to copy when blown up to a bigger size. So Ric explained a very old technique to me, working with a badger brush. The dry brush softens the edges of the fresh applied color to the cardboard. I was fascinated by that technique. The same night at home I tested it and finished my first three backgrounds in a size twelve field. They became the first designs to define the final style of the movie.

© Disney Enterprises, Inc.

In 2006, I had a chance to go to China for the first time. I was invited to give some lectures at two universities. It was amazing. All the students I met knew our movie and liked it. And I could see some of the beautiful treasures this country had to offer. I visited more than ten years after I started work on the film.

There are different ways to lead the eye to the center of interest. It depends on what the story requires. You may have to show important detail surrounding the character; it can be some secondary action or a few elements in the background that have to be arranged.

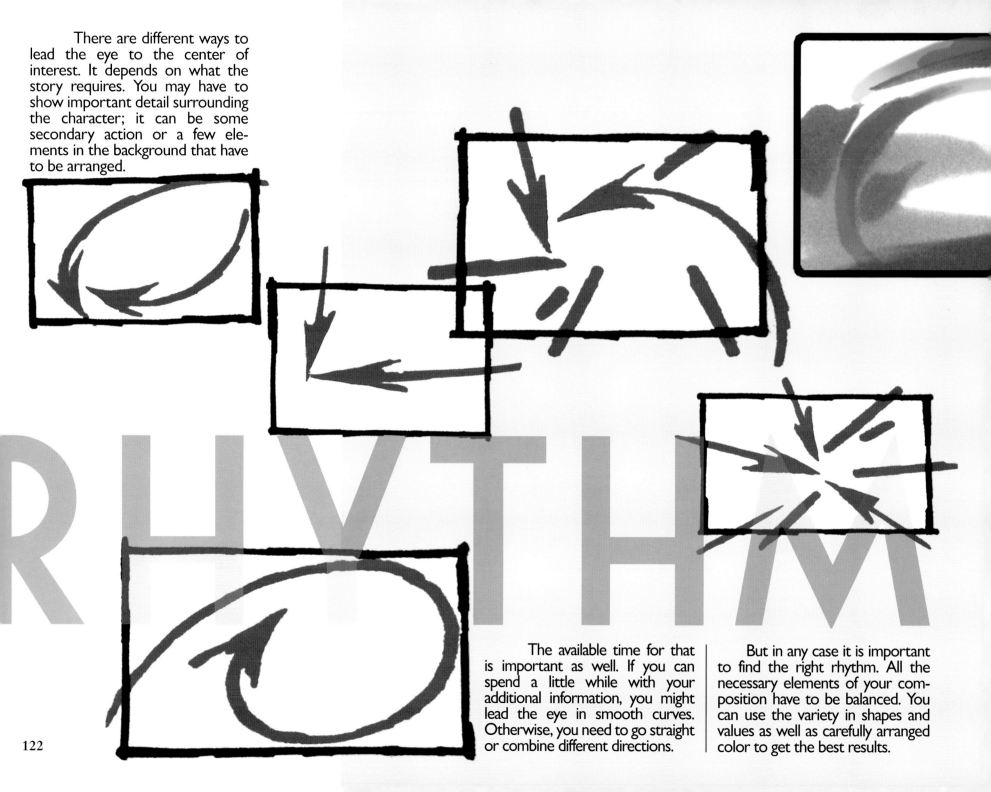

The available time for that is important as well. If you can spend a little while with your additional information, you might lead the eye in smooth curves. Otherwise, you need to go straight or combine different directions.

But in any case it is important to find the right rhythm. All the necessary elements of your composition have to be balanced. You can use the variety in shapes and values as well as carefully arranged color to get the best results.

The idea is a rhythm of the best-balanced design elements and camera arrangements along with a well-choreographed action. The next important step is to connect all different scenes in a sequence. Their rhythm creates the visual language of your movie.

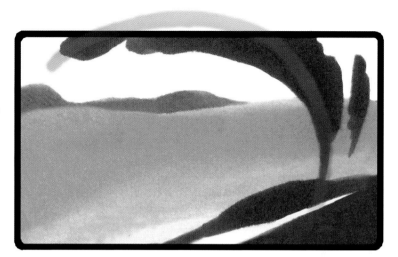

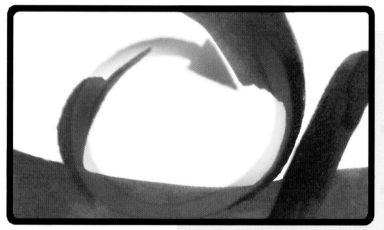

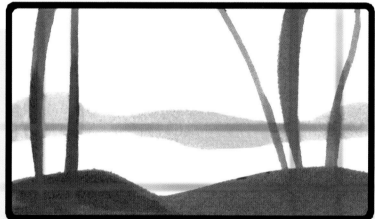

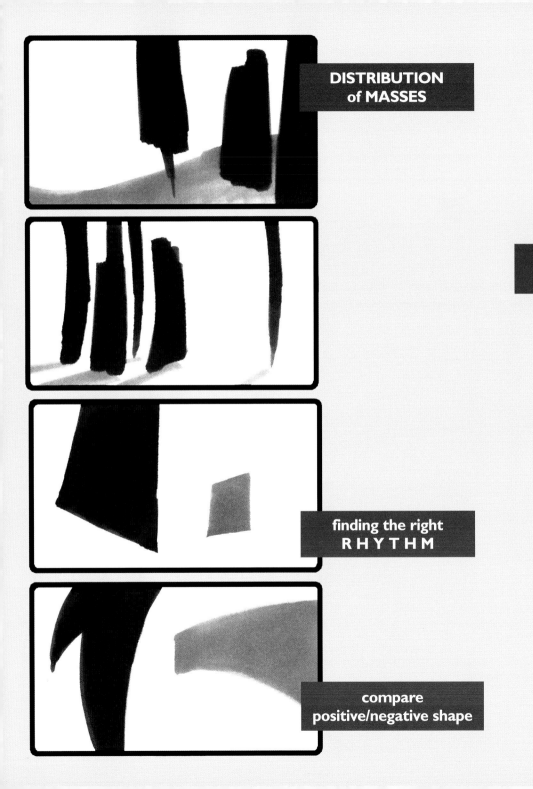

DISTRIBUTION of MASSES

finding the right
R H Y T H M

**compare
positive/negative shape**

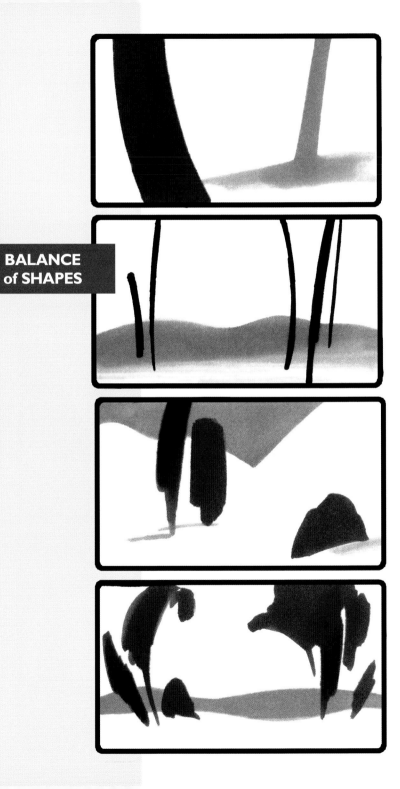

BALANCE of SHAPES

These are some simplified composition studies using all different ingredients to find the right rhythm. Characters are not included. In the next chapters, I will show you more examples on how to find the right composition of environment and action.

big studios of the past decided to have one artist design the look of the film and then have the others follow.

Most of the time a designer was chosen out of the team to come up with that style, and in some cases, an artist from the outside was hired when his style fit the story. For example, in the thirties, they hired Gustaf Tenggren and Kay Nielsen for *Snow White and the Seven Dwarfs* and *Fantasia*, and more recently Gerald Scarfe for *Hercules*. Walt Disney even had Salvador Dali work on a short film concept that was finished (after a long pause) only a few years ago.

In the early years, most of the larger studios had their own distinctive style; MGM's *Tom and Jerry* shorts; Warner Bros. *Looney Tunes* shorts; Fleischer's

Most animated movies today have their own style. Short films from independent filmmakers especially show unusual visuals. A lot of them are experimenting to find a new look. In a way, all these films are personal pieces of art, and an artist has his own style.

When it comes to bigger productions and animated feature films, that definition is a bit more complicated. In this case, the film is not the showpiece of a single artist; it is the combined effort of many artists.

To avoid a confusing mixture of different artistic handwritings, the

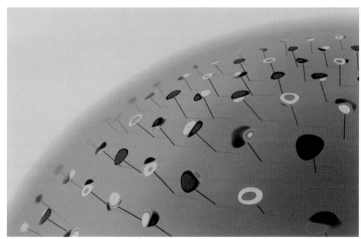

Popeye shorts from Paramount; Disney's *Silly Symphonies*, as well as the Mickey, Donald and Goofy shorts; and later, the Hanna-Barbera series.

It was not just the diversity of the characters starring in these shorts; it was the look that made them immediately recognizable.

127

One of the most important designers was Maurice Noble for Warner Bros. He created a style that influenced a lot of other designers. There were other important designers and painters such as Jules Engel, John Hubley, Saul Bass; and at Disney, Mary Blair, Ken Anderson and Eyvind Earle.

They were influenced by modern art, as well as by illustrators like Ronald Searle and The Provensens. And they influenced each other. After UPA started to produce highly stylized shorts in the early fifties, a whole revolution in the look of animated movies happened, even at Disney with shorts such as *Toot, Whistle, Plunk and Boom* and *Paul Bunyan.*

Around the world, some fantastic-looking shorts were the result of that development too. Films such as *The Great Jewel Robbery* and *Don Quixote* from the Zagreb Studio; or, Hubley's *Adventures Of An** and *Moonbird*; in Italy Bozzetto's *Sr. Rossi* series; and France's Paul Grimault and the Halas-Batchelor shorts from London.

The variety is even bigger today with so many commercials, movie titles and the Internet. And let us not forget all the different techniques such as puppet, clay- and CG-animation.

I hope that films of the future will continue to look interesting and will inspire new generations of filmmakers, and hopefully, art will remain more important than technique.

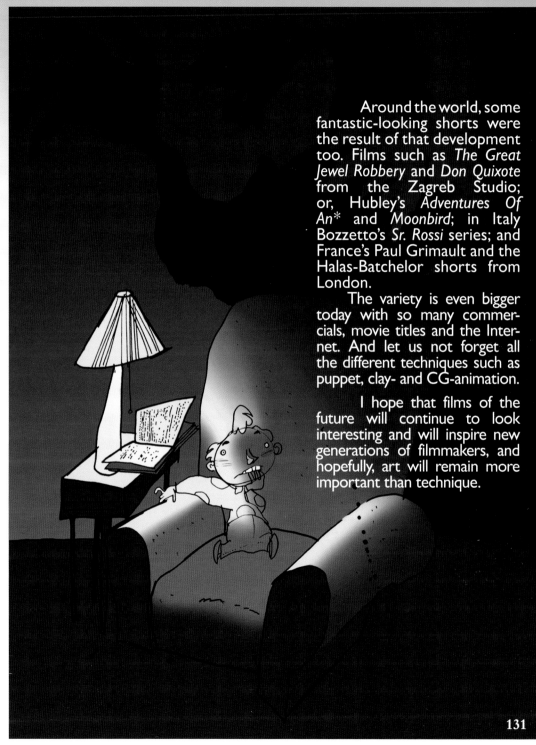

HAWAII

It must have been right after *Mulan* that I first saw Chris Sanders' children's storybook of *Lilo & Stitch*. There was no doubt that it was made for animation!

I was involved for a short time with a few location designs and ideas for interesting compositions. Together, with Ric Sluiter, the art director for *Mulan*, I went for a week to Kauai, one of the most beautiful Hawaiian Islands, to do some research. Ric painted while I explored the different beaches and villages, shooting several hundred slides.

What an island! My first time in Hawaii I loved it so much that I came back a year later with my wife.

The final film had a lot of that charm that I felt when I first came to the island. It was just the perfect place for the story.

And the watercolor style for the backgrounds added the final touch. Maybe for the last time, the old traditional-style watercolor art from the beautiful *Silly Symphonies*: *Elmer Elephant*, *Farmyard Symphony* and *Three Little Wolves*, which was recreated by the *top*-background team in Florida, came back to the screen. In my opinion it is a masterpiece.

133

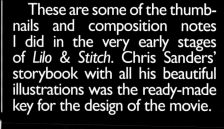

These are some of the thumbnails and composition notes I did in the very early stages of *Lilo & Stitch*. Chris Sanders' storybook with all his beautiful illustrations was the ready-made key for the design of the movie.

moving shadows
as texture

light and shadows
defining shapes

characters walking
in and out of shadow

reflection

The lights and darks of any color are called *values*. Normally these values are the result of light in nature. Where there is a lot of light, you get the lightest value — *white*; in the darkest shadow areas you get *black*. There is of course a scale of mid-values in different shades of grey. We reduce these middle tones to only three. It makes them easier to work with.

There are different ways to arrange scaled value steps in your sketch. Define the foreground, one or two middle ground areas, and then the background. In case you want to arrange the values realistically, your foreground might be the darkest, and your background the lightest tone. But even in nature you will find a situation where the sky is the darkest value and a middle-ground the lightest.

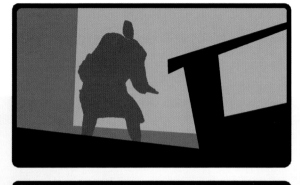

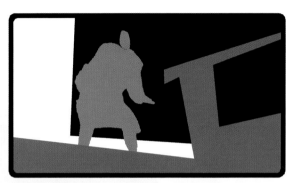

You should know what you want to design without following the rules of nature. To achieve the desired result, a scary moment or a romantic scene, you choose the best arrangement of values.

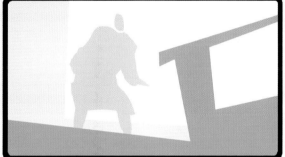

In these simple sketches, I want to show you the different options you have. You choose a combination because it is the best interpretation of a story situation. And don't forget, these sketches are not black & white. They define color. Use them as a starting point to determine the atmosphere, and then add the colors following your value range. This makes it much easier to create depth in your design, along with the right mood. And it is better to stage your character that way. You can see in these sketches different ways of making the action read.

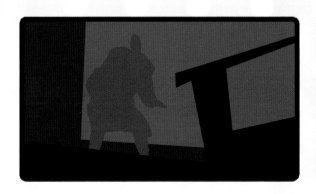

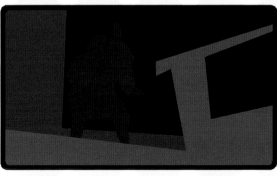

COLOR

Henri Matisse said, "When I choose a color it is not because of any scientific theory. It comes from observation, from feeling, from the innermost nature of the experience in question."

That worked well for Matisse. However, it doesn't hurt to know a little bit about the scientific background of why to use them, especially when color is such an important part of our business.

Color should be used to create specific moods. Of course our cultural background plays a significant role in that. Countries closer to the equator are more colorful in all ways than countries in the northern parts. Yet nearly everywhere around the world the same rules can be applied. Certain cool colors calm down the emotions, while hot colors create aggression in emotions. These colors can be used in different combinations to create different atmospheres. Psychologists and interior designers know how to use them together to achieve specific results. History will show you that dictators knew (and know) about the manipulative powers of color.

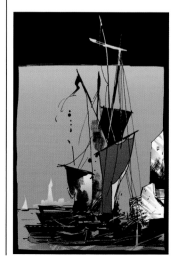

In the film business, especially in our area of animated films, it is not necessarily a good idea to use color because "it looks so nice!" Of course we could start a discussion about taste, but putting that aside, there are rules that have been created over the past eighty years. And it is best to study these rules so as not to repeat past mistakes.

The color in our films corresponds with specific events in the story, and just as there is an "emotion/action curve," there should be a "color mood curve." The dictates of the color palette will begin with the different seasons that the film takes place during, as well as the times of the day, weather situations, and interior/ exterior locations within the story.

For example, a love scene will need different colors than a suspense scene. At the end of the film, the color is especially important to build up the climax.

And just as music is a substantial ingredient used to establish the mood of the story, the proper colors and color combinations are just as important. Sequences need to be designed in "color-chapters" and "color-transitions" between the different sequences have to be developed. Normally, transitions are designed to be smooth; however, contrasting colors next to each other (from one sequence to the next and even from scene to scene) help indicate dramatic story changes that may occur and also helps create the appropriate emotional response.

Analyzing some of the older masterpieces that Disney has created such as *Bambi*, *Pinocchio*, *Fantasia* or *101 Dalmatians*, it is obvious how well-planned every single detail was, especially the color! Unlike today where our eyes are being hurt by tasteless experiences in the world of television, most specifically in the

world of children's programming. The color of the "good old days" was something very special, especially after the black & white years. Color meant something different back then, and it had to be used carefully. A lot of time was spent making sure it was used right! And I am not talking about realistic colors. This was the Hollywood "dream factory" using all the tricks. Every color was chosen for the special effect it had on the audience.

© Disney Enterprises, Inc.

In *The Sorcerer's Apprentice*, the color fades to black & white when Mickey destroys the broom. The color slowly returns to the rhythm of the music as the life returns within the broken wooden pieces.

Bambi shows us how masterfully transitions between color-chapters can be done. Just look at the beautiful scenes that were created solely to fill the gaps between late summer and the first snow of the winter.

Or in *The Three Caballeros*, fresh complementary color combinations create a happy atmosphere that conjures up the images of a South American carnival.

Peter Pan opens with the more subdued colors of Victorian England, only to transform into the complete opposite once we enter the world of Neverland.

140

In the mid-1950s, with a team of the best artists and thirty years of experience, the Disney studio created two more masterpieces: *Lady and the Tramp* and *Sleeping Beauty*. In *Lady and the Tramp*, color was more of a realistic mind. Depending on the mood of the sequence, the color was either fresh or tinted. With the latter, a very unique style was created by master artist Eyvind Earle. Elements of medieval European art were combined with Persian miniatures. Color was used very carefully because of the extensive number of layers used in the multi-plane camera and the immense amount of detail in the backgrounds. It is amazing that the characters read at all times in front of the "miniature masterpieces" and, on closer inspection, you will see that there is a clear "color-curve" throughout the whole of these films.

The rules that apply for background color choices also apply to character color choices. In comparing the villain-characters in the Disney films, you will find many similarities. There are sharp contrasts and lots of black with red or purple. "Heroes" are more down to earth with friendlier colors that are mixed with greys. Comic characters are often made up of pure fresh colors. Younger characters have different colors than older ones...the list is endless.

It is well worth your time to study films while knowing all of this. As a result, you will begin to understand why certain films are more successful than others, and why we make the choices we do when it comes to color.

ALASKA

AGAIN

When I worked on *Balto*, which was set in Alaska in the early nineties, I needed a lot of reference. The German Alps were the snowiest mountains I had ever seen.

But Alaska looked like this huge cold desert, with endless forests, big mountains, wild rivers – pure nature. *The Brother Bear* story was set back in time about ten thousand years ago, right after the Asian hunters crossed the then existing land bridge between Asia and Alaska. Today it is the Bering Strait.

As far as I remember, I was the first visual artist to work on the new project, which means the story was miles away from the end product. It was very mystical, with a grandmotherly character who was spiritually connected to a raven. Even the relationship between the brothers was different. Anyway, I was supposed to collect lots of "moody" ideas.

We had a four-day-long working session in Florida, I remember, with Harald Siepermann from Germany, and Terryl Witlatch who worked for ILM. Terryl did these incredible action drawings of bears and other animals, showing every single bone and muscle function. Harald

added his cartoony sense for the characters. And then there was Aaron Blaise and Bob Walker, the director team. Aaron was a master painter and incredible draftsman. Bob had been head of layout on *Mulan* and has a good sense for vistas. Not to forget Alex Kupershmidt, master animator and amazing draftsman, as well as Rune Brandt, a very young Danish artist with a brilliant cartoony sense. I will never forget those few days. It was a tour de force. We probably did altogether a thousand drawings.

Looking back, I wish we could have done something like that for all the other projects as well. We did not just do some sketches for the characters; complete sequences were developed and relations between characters clarified. There was a lot of electricity in that room, man! It was a good time, and I needed that. Because after a few weeks, I got the assignment to look after *Wild Life* and help them out of the visual mess it was stuck in.

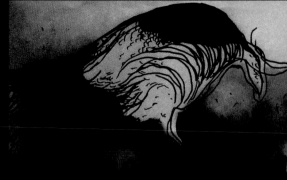

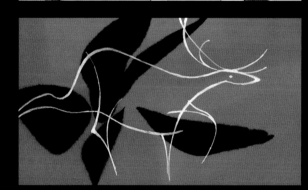

In very early versions of the script of *Brother Bear*, there was a dream-sequence. One of my favorite dream- or nightmare-sequences in animation is the "Pink Elephants" in *Dumbo*.

I wanted to create something similar, mixing ancient cave paintings with modern painting styles: Lascaux meets Picasso, Oldenburg, Braque, Rauschenberg and Chagall. Could have been fun...

Roger Allers, who had co-directed *The Lion King* and directed *The Emperor's New Groove*, was assigned in late 2000 to do *The Little Matchgirl*. He asked me to come up with some inspirational designs.

That Hans Christian Andersen story with the very sad ending was my favorite when I read the fairy tales for the first time as a child. I was excited to get involved, although for a short time only and unfortunately without any impact on the final look in the end. But anyway, there was reason enough to study some amazing Russian painters of the nineteenth

city of St. Petersburg where the story takes place.

The time of the year was around Christmas with lots of snow and dark nighttime sequences. Somehow I wanted to make the characters look Russian, which led me to study a lot of Nicolai Fechin's and other Russian painters' portrait paintings. The right look of winter costumes was important as well. But a big problem was the little girl. She was supposed to look very beautiful in her poor beggar clothing. I gave her a bit of an Asian look. We could not find an agreement about the final look during the few weeks I was working on it. And then someone else took over and I

© Disney Enterprises, Inc.

Here are my story-board thumbnails for the opening title of *Wild Life*.

150

At the beginning of 1999, I was asked to help on a project that a small team of artists with two new directors had started about two years before. They had major stylistic problems and I was supposed to fix them and then return to *Brother Bear*. The title of that project was *Wild Life*.

After a short time I realized that the style was not the only problem; the story was an even bigger one. And that did not change until the very end!

But I was fascinated by the basic stylistic ideas; they were just not organized. And the artists in the team were some of the best I had worked with so far. I liked the chaotic work environment so much that I stayed for over two years, all the way to the bitter end.

It was the first pure CG movie Disney ever had in preproduction. It was my first as well, so I had a lot to learn.

I had a chance to work with some amazing artists; Buck Lewis in Character Design; Dean Gordon, head of Background Design; Mac George, the best Layout Stylist; Jim Finn, Background Design; Mitch Bernal, 3-D Layout; Umesh Shukla, CG-Supervisor; and Kent Melton, Maquette Sculptor. Of course there were top 3-D Modelers and 3-D Animators as well. And for a short time, we had a Fashion Designer for the crazy futuristic costume look. The style we developed was a very modern mixture influenced by all major pop artists and abstract painters like Steward Davis, as well as the most modern architects and furniture designers.

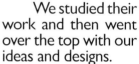

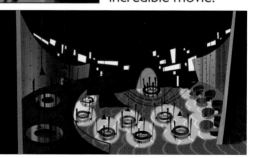

We studied their work and then went over the top with our ideas and designs.

The final look of the major areas in the story looked breath-taking, together with the very unusual character designs. It could have been an incredible movie.

It was a very sad moment when it went into turnaround. Somehow we had hoped the story would be fixed under a new leadership. Everybody loved our CG-test scenes. Anyway, it is history now.

The whole project seemed to be a big secret in the animation world. Probably because nothing had ever been published about it. I wish there could be a *The Art Of...* book one day. There were thousands of designs done by so many different artists; I remember Buck Lewis created more than one thousand character sketches. I did about five hundred, not to count the hundreds of environment and color sketches, and even more texture designs.

I will always remember these most creative years in my career, together with some of the most talented artists.

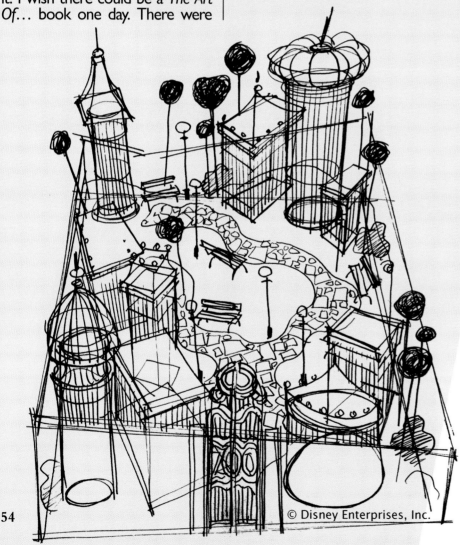

Anyway, the dream of a new art form-piece was over and I started to explore new ideas and looks along with Umesh Shukla, who had been head of CG on *Wild Life*. He is from India and has a background in Graphic Design as well. It was very helpful, as he knew everything about art and everything about the latest in technology.

From the very beginning, I remember him telling me, "Never think about how we might solve that look problem; in the end, design whatever you want. I will make it work."

That sounded incredible – no limitations! We worked for a while on a complete new look for a Florida project called *My Peoples*, now shelved as well. I tried to mix all different American painter styles together; especially those of Thomas Hart Benton and Grant Wood. Their very unique landscape composition as well as an interesting use of lots of textures looked very appealing and new to me. And we studied Bill Peet's children's books and his way of using crosshatching to create textures. Umesh came up with a 3-D crosshatched world. The problem was it looked too spiky and we somehow needed to get rid of that artificial technical feel.

154

It became even worse when Umesh and I started to develop a short film for a planned new version of *Fantasia*. My idea was to show abstract art of the last 70 years, combined in a simple story about a bird that doesn't fit into a bird society, kind of a non-conformist dreamer. We did CG tests with 3-D paintings in the style of Klee, Picasso, Miro and Matisse.

© Disney Enterprises, Inc.

What we had tried to do was create a marriage between traditional and CG animation, and to create a look using new technology that had been impossible to even dream about some years before. We wanted to come up with a new art form. But, probably it was too much art.

© Disney Enterprises, Inc.

It looked like a new era had already started – the CG-era. The next project I was offered to work on was again planned as a 3-D movie, but, I could not get used to the idea of designing another "plastic" look. Fortunately, I was the first artist to get involved in that new project, which was *Fraidy Cat*, so I could design with no limitations.

165

The story outline and the first treatment looked very promising. It was a little bit of a Hitchcock crime story about a cat and a parrot in London. Somehow, it reminded me of *101 Dalmations*, one of my favorite movies.

What I tried to do was a combination of 2-D and 3-D. Everything was supposed to be built 3-dimensionally, but would look flat in the end. Only a moving camera would reveal that there was an optical illusion.

I used a lot of textures for the different "flat"-design elements, but the textures had nothing in common with the material they were supposed to show. You can see a little bit of that in the designs on these pages. To get that look I had to design some thousand different brushes, which became an obsession over the years.

In a way, I had tried to do what I had always done in the past; if I did not like a certain idea, I modeled it into something similar that I could live with. Anyway, CG had a promising future with the fast developing technology. My only hope is that more artists get involved in the decision making of the bigger studios. It might help the artistic quality of future movies.

DECISION

It is something you always have to do in your personal life. Nobody teaches you, you have to learn it by yourself. One of the most important and difficult things in the design process is to decide that now is the moment my design is finished. That can be determined after 10 seconds or 10 hours.

You also have to decide about the choice of technique you are going to use, depending on the time you have, the budget and the subject. Is a small sketch enough or does it have to be a bigger illustration? Today, creating the artwork with computer software makes it much easier. Size is unimportant and you can work 10 times as fast as with traditional techniques. I remember very often how painfully slow it was to cut masks for airbrushing, and then during the final touches the airbrush pistol sprayed some nice unwanted spots on your artwork.

I had experienced that it was impossible to duplicate the freshness and originality of a small sketch when I had to create a "nicer" version in a bigger format.

It was very hard in the "old days" to decide when the felt pen and airbrush color design on special marker paper was finally finished. If you overworked it, there was unfortunately no undo button.

But with all of its advantages, technology today can give you some headaches as well. Painting software offers so many little tricks, so many filters, nice gradients and easy changes of color that you could actually work on the same piece of art forever.

Sometimes you accidentally come up with results you would have never dreamed of. That's the dangerous part. Most of the time experiments like that lead away from your original concept. It is a good decision to stick with that idea and not to get lost and sidetracked with the temptations of technology. And a good recipe for me always was, look at the artwork the next day. If it still looks good then you can live with it.

MAKING

It's so much more fun to design your own movies. Unfortunately, there is never enough time to do that when you are involved in your day-to-day job. Because nobody tells you what you have to do to please everybody upstairs, you have the pure freedom and can create looks you always wanted to explore. Usually artists are very critical toward themselves, so it is quite challenging to come up with something you, as your own client, like.

The title *Own Projects* is a little bit misleading; better would be *Your Own Crazy Ideas* nobody will ever want to produce. That's OK. I always created these imaginary projects to find ways to escape the sometimes boring "income"-work.

Another interesting thing is that you never finish your own dream projects. You create tons of designs until something interrupts the process. You stop for a while and then follow a new idea. But usually after a while you return to the drawer where you collect all the unfinished future Oscar nominations. I go through all my old stuff once in a while, sometimes after several years. It's a bit nostalgic at first, but then you dive right back into the creative process and change designs, add little things, improve characters. It's amazing. You realize how much you have learned during the intervening time. You improve on what you once thought was a masterpiece.

For a long time I used these challenging ideas to learn. I never enjoyed just reading about a new technique or a famous artist and his work. I wanted to get something out of this experience. You look at a new Picasso exhibition catalogue and you are so full of the work of this genius that you have to start sketching and painting with all your overflowing creativity. The same thing happens to me when I see a beautiful landscape or architecture, read a good story or see a well-done movie.

Recently I started teaching again after about 15 years. That is something else that kicks you forward, it is not really teaching, it is learning with the students. During that time you develop so many ideas that it is nearly impossible to remember them all after the lectures and work sessions. But one thing you keep with you is the energy and the motivation to create something new, as if you were back in school the way you were so many years ago.

175

When I am looking for a new style, I try to combine very unusual ingredients, occasionally even using computer-generated images as in this example. The different elements were created with a software called Artmatic, but then manipulated in Photoshop. Most of the time it is not quite clear what the end result will look like. That makes the process even more interesting.

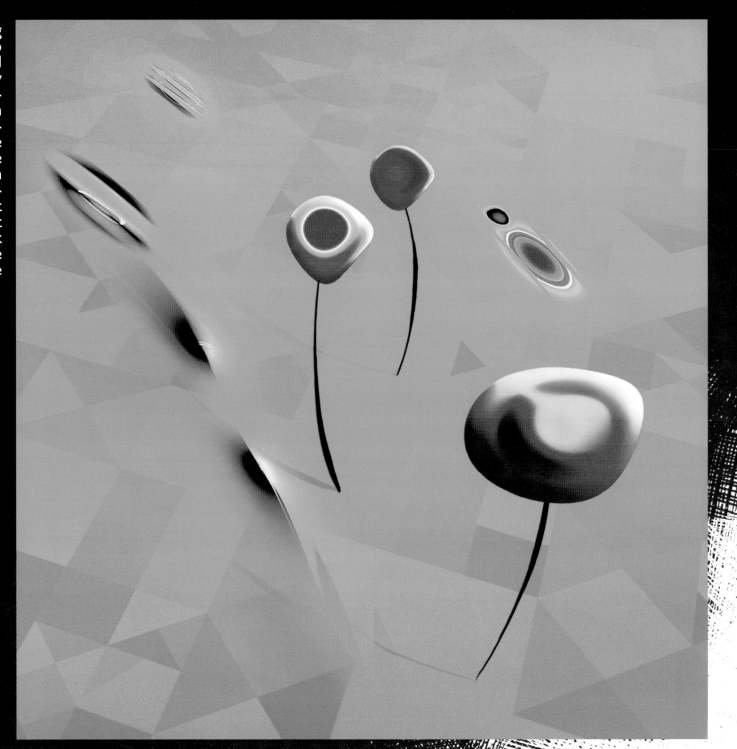

183

Back in 1989, I did a children's book that was never published. These are designs based on that book. After a few weeks of communicating with publishers I did not care for, I stopped all attempts to get the book printed.

Recently, I did some more work on it and now it looks like it will be an animated short. It is fun to do the designs with very loose brushwork and some Photoshop coloring.

184

This is a little bit of my personal history. In a way, that's how it all started! It says in one corner of this painting, 1965. I was 16 and I remember when and why I did this little style-study. I had seen an animated theatrical short in front of a live action feature film. For a long time I tried to find out about the studio that had produced it, I guess it must have been Zagreb Studio. The style of the backgrounds were fascinating. I found it very unusual because I was used to more realistic looking scenery in the older Disney movies. As soon as I was home, I tried to copy what I had seen and it changed my preferences in animation for a long time. From then on, I was more attracted to the *Hubley* shorts, everything that came from Zagreb Studio, UPA and Lenica in Germany. Even today I am more attracted to very stylized movies and try to create something new and unusual all the time.

191

UNPRODUCTIVE

Yeah Baby....
9.23.98

A production designer is one of the department heads and has to attend meetings where decisions about the movie have to be made.

There are endless, sometimes never-ending meetings. You have to be in a lot of them: Story, workbook, brain trust, layout, background, color, effects and sweatbox meetings. I am sure I forgot a few.

You can imagine some of the drawings you do during that time are not always productive, but good for a fun break. Sometimes you are just over-creative and all that energy has to go somewhere.

I was very fortunate to have had a chance to work with some very funny artists in this business. One of them was Barry Cook, who directed *Mulan* together with Tony Bancroft.

Barry and I attended hundreds of meetings about the look of the film, especially very early meetings via satellite link with the Florida studio. And there were a lot of funny sketches besides our work stuff. Here is a collection of some of them…

193

THE MASTERS

The backgrounds you will see on the next pages have never existed this way. The last time a cameraman saw them like this was when he checked the picture for shooting through the viewfinder of the multiplane camera.

The images that you see here were painted in several layers on glass to create depth.

After the scenes were shot and checked, the glass was scraped off, cleaned and prepared for the next set of paintings.

I always wanted to see these masterpieces in their full size because you only see a small part of the full-sized background at one time in the movie.

196

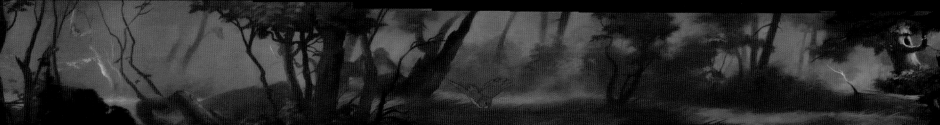

Here is what I wrote down after a tour through the camera department:

There were three rooms with 5 m high ceilings and three multiplane cameras, including one very old camera stand that had been used first in the thirties. On a big shelf they stored a lot of different-sized glass levels from older movies, foregrounds about 18×24 cm, the final lowest BG's about 40×60 cm. Every single level could be moved east/west, as well as north/south.

On the walls were huge cupboards with light controlling devices. The intensity of the light had to be increased the further you went down through all the levels since they had to compensate for the thickness of the glass levels.

In the old days, it took them about four days to mount and prepare one scene. The single-glass levels were about 100 kg (250 pounds) and had to be carried by four men. Then it took another three days to shoot the scene. Scenes with effects such as shadows, fire, water or snow were especially complicated and time consuming. They had to shoot most of them with masks (upper lights/lights from below). The water effect was done with a special glass level that had bubbles built-in to create the out-of-focus/in-focus water effects. Only one of these glasses was left. The same results were achieved later with rubber-cement glue on cells. Shadows were done by shooting the scenes twice, 30%/70% or 50%/50%; the first with the black shadow on cell, the second time without. The result was transparency. Fire was always a double or triple shot with different out-of-focus exposures for the glowing effect. Snow was filmed in live action with falling corn flakes in slow motion and then hard-contrast copied into the final scene. But the most complicated thing was to match the different levels and the animation on them. Up to eight people were working at the levels and camera with more on checking the exposure sheets.

The lower the animation level, the lighter the colors of the characters had to be, to match the increasing darkening effect of the thick glass. We saw in the Color Department special instructions for that. Amazing! During the production of *Snow White and the Seven Dwarfs*, the exposure time was about 20 seconds with a very small aperture because of the depth of field. With better technology they could lower it down to 8–10 seconds during the production of *Peter Pan*. Imagine, there are 24 frames per second! It took 4 minutes of pure shooting time for 1 second of film. That explains why there are only a few multiplane shots in these old masterpieces. It was just too time consuming and expensive.

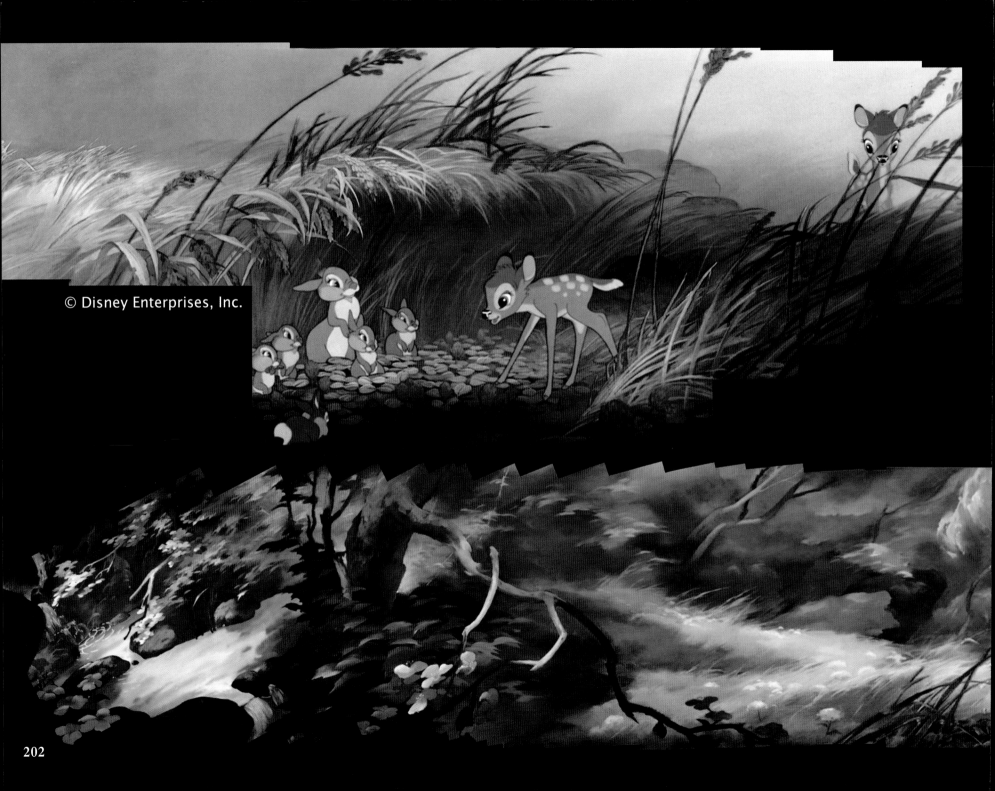

This is for everybody who wants to learn from the masters. With image capture software you can grab very precise key frames of camera pans. These frames can be mounted together and touched up a bit in Photoshop to recreate nearly the identical original background that was used for the film. I guess not too many people know that in the case of *Bambi*, only a few backgrounds are left in the Disney archives. Most of the film's scenes were several layer multiplane combinations, which means that the different foreground and middle-ground layers had to be painted on glass. That's how the incredible depth and focus effects were achieved. The only painting technique that could get the soft washes of the foliage and grass in the

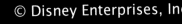

forest, as well as the snow and burning forest towards the end, was oil painting. Now the sad part – it was war time, the second world war, and resources were short. To save glass and costs, the oil painted BG's were scraped off the glass layers and the glass was reused for the next multilayered painting. There is only one complete multilayered glass set with oil painted trees that was used in the Disney documentary *Tricks of Our Trade*, produced in February 1957 for the Disney tv series. In one part of the show Walt Disney explains the multiplane camera and they simulate the work on the opening shot of *Bambi*, explaining in detail how the depth was achieved with all the different glass layers.

INDEX